LawyerLife

Finding a Life and a Higher Calling in the Practice of Law

Carl Horn III

Cover design by Andrew Alcala

The materials contained herein represent the opinions of the author and should not be construed to be the actions of the American Bar Association unless adopted pursuant to the bylaws of the Association.

Nothing contained in this book is considered as the rendering of legal advice, and readers are responsible for obtaining such advice from their own legal counsel. The book is intended for educational and informational purposes only.

Library of Congress Control Number: 2003105440

ISBN: 1590312481

www.ababooks.org

CONTENTS

ACKNOWLEDGMENTS

I am deeply indebted to those who have helped with this long project, which began with several articles and grew ultimately into this book. It has been a labor of love, but I certainly could not have done it without them.

First, there are the pioneers who foresaw and wrote about troubling trends in the legal profession—discontent, quality-of-life concerns, and plummeting public respect, for example—before most of us understood their scope or significance. Yale Law School Dean Anthony Kronman (*The Lost Lawyer: Failing Ideals of the Legal Profession*), Ambassador Sol Linowitz (*The Betrayed Profession: Lawyering at the End of the Twentieth Century*), Benjamin Sells (*The Soul of the Law: Understanding Lawyers and the Law*), and Harvard Law Professor Mary Ann Glendon (*A Nation Under Lawyers*) published their groundbreaking books in 1993 and 1994. I am indebted, and indeed the legal profession is indebted, to each of these authors for having the courage and wisdom to speak out as clearly and forcefully as they did.

Although many law professors are properly criticized for not caring about the real-life practice of law, we are indebted as a profession to those who do. Here I think of the intelligent, helpful contributions of Professors (or Deans) Marc Galanter, Thomas Palay, Deborah Rhode, David Link, Patrick Schiltz, Walter Bennett, Peter Kutulakis, Roger Schechter, Carl Bogus, Lawrence Krieger, Roy Stuckey, Alan Dershowitz, Lawrence Joseph, Bruce Winnick, and James Alfini. Of course, there are others who should be on this list, but these are some of the academic voices that have shaped my own thoughts and priorities.

Next I think of the practicing lawyers who have written with style, and with enough humor to make the message constructive, about their own less-than-perfect experiences. Walt Bachman (*Law v. Life: What Lawyers Are Afraid to Say About the Legal Profession*), George Kaufman (*The Lawyer's Guide to Balancing Life and Work: Taking the Stress Out of Success*), Cameron Stracher (*Double Billing: A Young Lawyer's Tale of Greed, Sex, Lies, and the Pursuit of a Swivel Chair*), and Merit Bennett (*Law and the Heart: A Practical Guide to Successful Lawyer/Client Relationships*) all come to mind. You all broke the ice—putting the emperor on notice that at least some knew he was getting pretty close to naked—and for this key contribution the entire profession is in your debt.

The growing ranks of helping professionals offering their services to lawyers, some of whom are themselves lawyers, are both encouraging and deserving of public commendation. Those who come to mind, most of whom are cited or recommended in the following pages, are Benjamin Sells, George Kaufman, Amiram Elwork (author of *Stress Management for Lawyers*), Dr. Preston Munter, Ralph McFall, Rob Lehman, Hindi Greenberg, Dr. Sara Eddy, Leona Vogt, Fran Shellenberger, and Richard Gottfried.

No list of written contributions to the contemporary legal profession would be complete without recognizing Steven Keeva, Assistant Managing Editor of the *ABA Journal*. His book, *Transforming Practices: Finding Joy and Satisfaction in the Legal Life*, and his many articles with like themes, have been liberally quoted in these pages and for good reason. In addition to being a gifted writer and introducing us to a number of lawyers who *are* professionally fulfilled (John McShane, Arnie Herz, John McQuiston, and Richard Halpert, for example), Keeva's underlying message is precisely what many lawyers most need to hear.

Few authors are as fortunate as I am when it comes to top-rate editorial support. Beginning with my long-term friend Bryan Kay, the ABA's Director of Publishing, and continuing with the outstanding assistance of Director of New Product Development Adrienne Cook, the support, suggestions, and co-labors of ABA Publishing have been superb.

Here on the home front I am equally appreciative of the many hours my secretary, Susan Williamson, has devoted to this project. Not only has Susan typed and revised many hundreds of pages without a single complaint, she has zealously promoted the book—and, far more importantly, the principles it advocates—to many of the lawyers who have passed through our chambers. Susan, however your lawyer listeners responded to your importuning, I hope you realize how much

I appreciate not only your technical talents, but also your generous and enthusiastic attitude.

David Grigg, who practiced law for a number of years before becoming my career law clerk about three years ago, is another indispensable contributor to this project, and indeed, to all my work. He is brilliant, energetic to a fault, and has all that I lack in computer expertise. He is also a wonderful friend who regularly provides the kind of personal and spiritual support that dollars cannot buy. I would literally be lost without him.

One of the legal profession's time-tested practices, often neglected when billable hours requirements and the bottom line dominate law firm "values," is the mentoring of younger lawyers by older, more experienced ones. It is a practice heartily advocated in this book, and therefore it seems appropriate to recognize here my first mentor and "boss," Joseph W. Grier, Jr. Mr. Grier graduated from Harvard Law School and returned to his hometown to practice just after World War II. Now in his 80s (and still going to the office almost every day), he is responsible for training some of Charlotte, North Carolina's finest lawyers (present company excluded). While I do not claim to be one of those, I do share their profound sense of appreciation for the careful, intelligent, and generous way he brought us along to professional maturity.

Although I have been interested in the issues addressed in this book for more than 25 years, and have been writing and speaking about them for more than a decade, I knew from the outset I had my blind spots and that it would be a challenge to communicate effectively a sufficiently broad message. For this reason, I sought input as the writing progressed from a number of reviewers with a wide variety of points of view and backgrounds. I am indebted to those who took the time to read and comment, undaunted by the thick packages I was sending, especially to those whose constructive criticism improved the final product.

Thanks especially—with sincere apologies to any I have neglected to mention—to Professors Mary Ann Glendon and Walter Bennett, Chief U.S. District Judge Graham Mullen, Walt Bachman, Rob Musser, Judge Bill Constangy, Will Esser, Patrick Horn, George Kaufman, Dr. Lee Stoffel, Everett Walker, John Clark (who is so capably chairing the ABA's lawyer assistance work as this is being written), Robert Turnbull, Judge Chase Saunders, David Shuford, Tim Murphy, and Jim Smith.

Finally, I am indebted to those of you who read earlier article-length versions of these themes. Some readers served as *de facto* editors, others wrote to compliment or encourage, and a few of you distributed or reprinted the earlier articles. Again, with apologies to any I have neglected to mention, heartfelt thanks to former ABA President Roberta Cooper Ramo, Dean Pat Hetrick, John Cunningham, Bill Olive, Judge Bob Johnston, Sanford Thompson, Larry Sitton, Rich Robertson, Steve Crihfield (whose passion is to persuade courts to adopt a "Vacation Policy" allowing litigators to make personal plans without fear of last-minute surprises), Joel Stoudenmire, Wendall Winn, Joe Condo, Jordan Furlong (editor of the Canadian Bar Association's *National* magazine, which reprinted an earlier article in English and French), and Neil Yarborough.

Thanks to one and all. I hope you enjoy the book you helped write, and that it encourages you and many others to keep up the good work—and live the good LawyerLife.

Carl Horn III
Charlotte, North Carolina

Part One

The Contemporary Practice of Law

CHAPTER 1

Law as a "High Calling"?

Recent books and articles about the legal profession paint a troubling picture. Although the optimism/pessimism mix and proposed remedies vary, many agree with Harvard Law Professor Mary Ann Glendon that the profession is in extremis—or, as she puts it, on "the edge of chaos."[1] Indeed, Yale Law School Dean Anthony T. Kronman ups the philosophical ante in *The Lost Lawyer: Failing Ideals of the Legal Profession,* diagnosing "a spiritual crisis" in which "the profession now stands in danger of losing its soul."[2]

Other notable commentators concur. Almost ten years ago Sol M. Linowitz, about to retire from a distinguished career in law, business, and government,[3] minced no words in *The Betrayed Profession: Lawyering at the End of the Twentieth Century.* Ambassador Linowitz's assessment, rich in historical example, laments the transformation of the profession he loved—and understood to be a high public calling—into an increasingly unprincipled, dollar-driven business.[4]

With the current prevalence of lawyer misery,[5] lawyer-bashing,[6] and lawyer jokes,[7] it is crucial that the legal profession rediscover the "high calling" and rekindle the ideals that are its prouder heritage. On the other hand, lest we appear hopelessly naive, before the law-as-a-high-calling flag can be credibly raised, two caveats are in order.

Caveat One: Polls, Surveys, and Opinions

Whether or not it is entirely deserved, the general public's low opinion of lawyers must be acknowledged and engaged. Even if much of the criticism is based on composite stereotypes or media hype of atypical cases, addressing negative perceptions is a necessary step toward reestablishing foundational ideals and restoring public respect for the legal profession.

Professor Roger E. Schechter accurately summarized relevant survey data in his 1997 article titled "Changing Law Schools to Make Less Nasty Lawyers":[8]

> The public does not think well of us. Lawyers are held in extraordinarily low regard by the public at large. In several recent surveys ranking public esteem of various professions, lawyers have scored near the bottom. One such poll revealed that 95 percent of Americans would not recommend that their sons or daughters enter the legal profession. The members of the profession are considered arrogant, confrontational, manipulative, and unscrupulous, to state just a few of the adjectives that can be said in polite company.[9]

Unhappily, polls and surveys conducted in the 1980s and 1990s confirm Professor Schechter's conclusions. For example, in a 1993 American Bar Association (ABA) poll, "out of nine professions, only lawyers (40 percent), stockbrokers (28 percent), and politicians (21 percent) scored minority favorability ratings."[10] The same year a *National Law Journal*/West Publishing Company poll found that almost a third of Americans believed lawyers were "less honest than most people."[11] In the ABA poll, only one in five considered lawyers to be "honest and ethical" and "the more a person [knew] about the legal profession and the more he or she [was] in direct personal contact with lawyers, the lower [his or her] opinion of them."[12]

A 1997 Harris poll produced similar results. Comparing the percentage of the public that regarded various occupations as "very prestigious" in 1977 and 1997, the "drop [in the percentage placing law in this category was] the biggest among occupations in the survey." The occupations considered more prestigious than law in the 1997 survey, and the percentages considering them "very prestigious" were doctor (52 percent), scientists (51 percent), minister/clergyman (45 percent), teacher (40 percent), engineer (32 percent), and athlete (21 percent). Lawyers, down from 36 percent in 1977, were tied with artists at 19 percent and 1 percentage point ahead of entertainers (18 percent).[13]

In a separate Harris poll, also conducted in 1997, law firm "leaders" received even lower marks. *National Law Journal* reporter Chris Klein summarized the findings of the second poll:

> Just 7 percent of respondents have "a great deal of confidence" in people who run law firms—dead last on a list of 14 such institutions. Leaders of

> the military placed first, garnering 37 percent, followed by medicine at 29 percent and the U.S. Supreme Court at 28 percent. One notch above those in charge of law firms were leaders of organized labor, in whom 9 percent of respondents said they had great confidence.[14]

Intending no slight to the wise and virtuous in their ranks, when public confidence in the leaders of organized labor is greater than their confidence in bar leaders, Houston, we have a problem.

On the other hand, as Stanford Law Professor Deborah L. Rhode reminds us in her provocative book, *In the Interests of Justice: Reforming the Legal Profession,* criticism of lawyers and their ancient craft is nothing new.[15] Indeed, when paid advocates first emerged over 2000 years ago, Seneca described our early forbears as "smothered by their prosperity," and Plato scorned their "small and unrighteous souls."[16] In *Utopia,* Sir Thomas More (1478–1535)—the Lord Chancellor of England deposed by King Henry VIII and, according to Catholic tradition, a patron saint of lawyers—specifically excluded all lawyers from his vision of the perfect society. Several hundred years later another Englishman, Samuel Johnson (1709–1784), sardonically quipped: "I do not care to speak ill of any man behind his back, but I believe the gentleman is an attorney."[17]

Alexis de Tocqueville's high view of early American lawyers notwithstanding,[18] Walter Bennett is correct that:

> The resentment of the power of lawyers is not new but is deeply embedded in our social history. American colonists brought with them from England a dislike of lawyers who, in the "old world," were part of the political and financial elite. . . . Lawyers were seen as part of an evil and unnatural apparatus that worked to repress and disenfranchise the common man and to undermine the ideal of a utopian republic.[19]

There are many historical examples of the antilawyer sentiment in early America, some of which are better for a hearty laugh than most lawyer jokes in current circulation. Consider, for example, the description of the Grafton County, New Hampshire population in its 1770 census report: "6,489 souls, most of whom are engaged in agriculture. . . . There is not one lawyer, for which we take no personal credit, but thank an Almighty and Merciful God."[20]

Less humorous but equally unequivocal is University of Wisconsin Law Professor Marc Galanter's summary of widespread antipathy toward lawyers during the same period and extending for at least 100 years:

> In the years following the revolution "there existed a violent universal prejudice against the legal profession as a class" and its members "were denounced as banded, as blood-suckers, as pick-pockets, as wind-bags, as smooth-tongued rogues. . . . The mere sight of a lawyer . . . was enough to call forth an oath." In the Jacksonian era and in the years after the rise of industrialism, there were strong currents of hostility to lawyers that are not outdone by contemporary lawyer bashing.[21]

Of course, it is not altogether fair to compare contemporary law practice to Greek or Roman, or even eighteenth- and nineteenth-century practice—before most American lawyers had attended law school, the first bar association had been formed, or standards for admission or ethical practice had been clearly established.[22] On the other hand, there is something strangely comforting in realizing that the current barrage of criticism is not without historical antecedent, particularly in light of the many laudable accomplishments of the profession—providing a majority of our presidents, for example—in the intervening years. If we survived the dismissive contempt of these earlier periods, earning public respect and even admiration from subsequent generations, why can our current choices not effect a similar transformation in future public opinion?

Historical perspective is also helpful in responding to specific criticisms. Most lawyers are now familiar with the concern—and an increasing percentage share it—that the "dignity and honor" formerly associated with our profession have been "contaminated with the spirit of commerce."[23] Many, however, will be surprised to learn that this particular charge was levied in 1895. In the 1930s, a period some commentators include in the "Golden Age" of lawyering in the United States, Supreme Court Justice Harlan Fisk Stone complained that pressures had already transformed many lawyers into "obsequious servants of business . . . tainted with the morals and manners of the marketplace. . . . "[24]

What we do with this criticism, from the ancient to the most recent poll and survey, may be less important than that we show good faith—and a measure of humility—in acknowledging it. In the eyes of many, the legal profession has lost its way. Have we? What *are* our higher, more-noble purposes in twenty-first-century America, and how might we better demonstrate these to a cynical public, which increasingly sees lawyers as "sharks" preying on the problems of others, or worse, as high-priced whores willing to do almost anything if the money is right?

These are unavoidable questions if we are to achieve what must be our goals: renewed ideals, a sense of "calling" in our work, and proud participation in a profession that has reclaimed—even in the eyes of the fickle public—its "dignity and honor."[25]

Caveat Two: No "Golden Age"

Much of the recent literature lamenting the legal profession's loss of character or status presumes there were earlier periods during which the bar more or less "had it together." Dean Kronman, for example, appears to favor a period spanning the ninteenth and twentieth centuries when "lawyer-statesmen," primarily from major cities, moved freely from successful law practices to periods of equally impressive public service. For Professor Glendon, who graduated from University of Chicago Law School in 1961 (where the famous Karl Llewellyn, father of the "legal realism" movement and author of *The Bramble Bush,* was one of her professors) and then practiced for a number of years before teaching law, the showcase period is roughly 1920 to 1960. Glendon highlights this period for emulation as a time "when lawyers were 'widely oriented . . . to a common set of ideals'; bar leaders consistently affirmed concepts of professionalism; associates who did good work were ordinarily rewarded with partnerships; [and] lawyers would subordinate considerations of economic gain to 'firm solidarity or to ideals of right conduct.'"[26]

Dean Kronman, Professor Glendon, and others are correct to highlight admirable qualities and practices of earlier periods, and indeed, any discipline hoping for a bright future neglects its past at great peril. On the other hand, as Professors Rhode and Gallanter also correctly instruct, it would be a mistake to consider any period a "Golden Age" or to apply recent critiques and criticism primarily as a call for return to the past.[27] We cannot turn back the clock—and might not be as pleased as expected if we could—although our own period may be becoming, as Gallanter has quipped, "the . . . Golden Age of nostalgia for the Golden Age of lawyering."[28]

There are two fundamental reasons why we must not allow future efforts to restore or reform the legal profession to devolve primarily into nostalgic longing to turn back the clock. First, whatever period is selected as a model, upon closer scrutiny we will discover that it had ample deficiencies and problems of its own. The legal profession has been, and continues to be, a work in progress. And second, comparing the large and diverse bar of the twenty-first century, and our increasingly varied and complex work arrangements, to the much smaller, more homogenous bar of any other period is to a substantial degree a comparison of apples to oranges.

Dean Kronman's "lawyer-statesmen" period would include, for example, the formation in 1870 of the Association of the Bar of the City of New York, the nation's first local bar association—but as it turns out, an organization that only welcomed the "decent part" of the practicing bar.[29] At the same time, writes legal historian Lawrence Friedman, "the odor of corruption" permeated the courtrooms of New York City,[30] "justice" was openly for sale in certain judicial chambers, and the practice of the "magnificent shyster," William F. Howe, notoriously flourished through regular "perjury, bribery, and blackmail."[31]

During the so-called "gilded age" of the late ninteenth and early twentieth centuries, Professor Glendon herself observes that "some of the bar's best and brightest made their reputations 'using every tactic in the book (and many that were not) to help bust unions, consolidate monopolies, and obtain favorable treatment' from corrupt judges."[32] As noted, strenuous criticism of those who were "commercializing" the legal profession also dates from this period,[33] compelling no less august a figure than Supreme Court Justice Louis Brandeis to warn lawyers, in 1903, "that they were losing public respect because they were also losing their commitment to public service and their moral independence from clients."[34]

Compared to the antilawyer attitude in certain quarters of colonial America and the open corruption in some segments of the bar in the late 1800s, the mid-twentieth century does appear to be a calm between the storms. What limited research exists indicates that the typical lawyer during this period, whether practicing in a major city or in a small town, was both professionally satisfied and held in relatively high public esteem. The latter was reflected in the almost heroic way lawyers were portrayed in the media during this period. Legal sociologist Marc Gallanter made this broad point in his 1998 article, "The Faces of Mistrust: The Image of Lawyers in Public Opinion, Jokes, and Political Discourse":

> The period around 1960 may well have been the historic high point of public regard for law and lawyers. It was certainly an era of favorable portrayal by the media. In movies such as *Witness for the Prosecution* (1957), *Anatomy of a Murder* (1959), *Compulsion* (1959), *Inherit the Wind* (1960), *Judgment at Nuremberg* (1961), and *To Kill a Mockingbird* (1962), and on television (*The Defenders* [1961–65], *Perry Mason* [1966–72]), lawyers ranged from the benign to the heroic. Steven Stark regards the lawyers portrayed in shows like *The Defenders* and *Owen Marshall* (1971–74) as "television's great benevolent authority figures. . . ." To Anthony Chase, the portrayals in films like *To Kill a Mockingbird* represent a complete integration of the virtuous-lawyer archetype in popular culture—an elaborated image unprecedented . . . [in] American mass cultural iconography.[35]

However satisfied or well regarded lawyers may have been during the halcyon 1960s, however, there are two basic reasons why the large and diverse bar of the present can glean only limited lessons from this happier, more stable period: simple math and a dramatic increase in diversity.

First, consider the numbers: In 1850, "there were according to one estimate, 21,979 lawyers in the country. . . . By 1880, there were perhaps 60,000 lawyers; by 1900, about 114,000."[36] This pattern of manageable growth continued until the mid-1960s when doubling size and diversity over a 20-year period had come to mean absorbing hundreds of thousands of new lawyers, and diversity of those entering the legal profession had dramatically increased. Between 1965 and 1985, for example, "the size of the profession doubled (from 300,000 to more than 600,000) as upwardly mobile young men and women swarmed to the nation's law schools."[37] By the early 1990s, lawyer ranks had grown to more than 750,000, and as this book is written, to around 1.1 million.[38]

Simply put, what may have "worked" when there were only a handful of lawyers in small to medium-sized towns—and even major city bars numbered only in the hundreds—cannot be successfully replicated for bars that now number in the thousands or even tens of thousands. While we are right to strive for a return to the civility and "professionalism" of earlier periods, the challenge is certainly exacerbated by the increase in the sheer number of lawyers. And, of course, lawyers who rarely or never see each other outside the workplace can hardly be expected to form the kind of personal relationships that were the building blocks of civility in the past.

Just as the number of lawyers has dramatically increased, so has the diversity of those entering the profession. Harry T. Edwards, former Chief Judge of the U.S. Court of Appeals for the District of Columbia, an African-American who entered the profession in 1965, poignantly illustrates why we must think again about nostalgia for the "good old days." Speaking at the 74th annual meeting of the American Law Institute in 1997, Judge Edwards rightly cautioned:

> I must say that I am highly skeptical of suggestions that we should look to the "good old days" to find cures for our profession's ills. In the "good old days," I could not have been a member of the federal bench. In fact, when I graduated from the University of Michigan Law School in 1965—with top grades, law review, and Order of the Coif honors—I could not get a job with most of the major law firms whose cases I now hear and decide. I recall interviews with several partners from prominent law firms who said that, although they were impressed with my record, their firms would not hire a "Negro." I, for one, am hardly enamored of the "good old days."[39]

Certainly, Judge Edwards would concur with the goals of the professionalism movement, particularly its call for a greater commitment to public service, but his words of caution about uncritical nostalgia must also be heeded.

In his tome *A History of American Law*, Professor Friedman traces the cultural, ethnic, and gender homogeneity of the bar back to its early American origins. At the beginning of the ninteenth century, lawyers in the most influential bars—New York and Philadelphia, for example—came "predominantly from families of wealth, status, and importance."[40] Although the mid-ninteenth century witnessed a higher percentage of new lawyers coming from the middle class—"sons of shopkeepers, clerks, small businessmen"[41]—the big Wall Street firms and the "little Wall Streets in other cities" continued to be "solid Republican, conservative in outlook, standard Protestant in faith, [and] old English in heritage" well into the twentieth century.[42] Much like the exclusive clubs to which most of the partners belonged, those regarded as outsiders—which included Jews, women, any ethnic minority, and most Catholics—simply "needed not apply."

Mary Ann Glendon's interview at Cravath, Swaine & Moore in the early 1960s is instructive—and probably not atypical. Like Judge Edwards, Glendon was a top graduate of an elite law school, but that was not enough to get a female foot in the door in those "good old days."

As Glendon, now a distinguished professor at Harvard Law School, recalls the reason given for her rejection:

> It was no use hiring me, a senior partner bluntly explained, because "I couldn't bring a girl in to meet Tom Watson [of IBM] any more than I could bring a Jew." The "golden age" was a time of shameless exclusionary practices.[42]

And this anecdote from the very period emulated for its "civility"! The increase in number and percentages of women entering the legal profession since Professor Glendon's ill-fated interview has been nothing short of dramatic. As one commentator expressed it, "When American law schools opened their doors in the fall of 1990, 53,000 women, about one-half the total enrollment, strode inside with their male colleagues. This figure is remarkable compared with 1966, when women were awarded a mere 3.5 percent of all law degrees conferred in the United States. . . ."[43]

The challenges—and, as we will see, the opportunities—presented by the increase in women in the profession will be addressed in future chapters. However, it should be noted here that this dramatic increase in women lawyers—beginning in the mid-1960s and expected to plateau at between 40 and 50 percent sometime in the next decade or two—is the single most compelling reason why even the successes of the past will have limited utility in our efforts to fashion a more promising future. This is true for two basic reasons. First, without succumbing to gender stereotype, the complex needs of our twenty-first-century workforce—looking for more-creative arrangements to balance profession and family, for example—bears little resemblance to those of what was essentially a male fraternity with mostly stay-at-home moms just a few decades ago. Second, addressing what Dean Kronman calls our "spiritual crisis" will require a healthy measure of what women have traditionally done better than men: building relationships, reconnecting with heart and healthy emotions, and striving for better balance generally.

The point here is not to dwell on the blind spots, or even the egregious sins of the past, which would serve little constructive purpose. Rather, we accept as fact "that historically the legal profession was exclusive by race and gender and to some degree social class,"[44] and then apply this knowledge in two basic ways. First, we avoid a simplistic response to contemporary problems; that is, we will use our historical awareness to escape the tempting illusion that there was a "golden age" to which we can or should return. And second, our current diversity will be kept clearly in mind as we consider what core values and ideals to affirm and what steps should be taken—as a profession and as individuals—to advance them.

The Best of the Past/Renewed Hope for the Future

Having acknowledged our critics and conceded the legal profession's somewhat mottled history, perhaps it will not strike even the cynical reader as self-serving if we now consider what is, or has been, "high" or "noble," or in the nature of a "calling," about the practice of law. Indeed, these brighter elements of our history are what Professor Rhode —in a book full of sharp and sweeping criticism of the contemporary profession—collectively calls "a broader truth."[45] As Professor Rhode explains, hers is:

> a book with a reform agenda, and its focus is more on what is wrong with lawyers than on what is right. But that emphasis should not obscure a broader truth. The legal profession is also responsible for much that is best in American democratic processes. Lawyers have been architects of a governmental structure that is a model for much of the world. And they have been leaders in virtually all major movements for social justice in the nation's history.[46]

Professor Carl T. Bogus, who practiced law in Philadelphia for eighteen years before joining a law faculty, makes a parallel point in his article—sanguinely and, we hope, inaccurately titled "The Death of an Honorable Profession":[47]

> [L]awyers enjoyed a special status from the very beginning of the Republic. Twenty-five of the fifty-two men who signed the Declaration of Independence were lawyers. Many highly regarded—even revered—figures were lawyers, among them Jefferson, Hamilton, Marshall, John Adams, and Daniel Webster. From 1790 to 1930, two-thirds of all U.S. senators and roughly half of all members of the House of Representatives were lawyers; since 1937, lawyers have made up between half and three-quarters of the Senate, more than half of the House, and more than 70 percent of all presidents, vice presidents, and members of the cabinet. At present [in 1996], the President and more than half of all U.S. senators and state governors are lawyers.[48]

Even if some of these lawyer politicians also brought a measure of disrepute to the profession—Presidents Nixon and Clinton, for example—this is an impressive record by any standard.

There was undeniably a degree of antilawyer sentiment present in early American society, as has been dutifully noted.[49] But that is not the whole story or the end of the story. French historian Alexis de Tocqueville, who toured America in 1831 and 1832, certainly reached a starkly different conclusion, describing lawyers in his famous treatise, *Democracy in America,* as the "only enlightened class *not* distrusted by the people."[50] As de Tocqueville reflected on the various forces at work in early America, searching for a counterbalance to what he regarded as potential dangers and excesses of a pure democracy, it was the nation's lawyers and judges in whom he placed most confidence.[51]

Of course, it is possible that de Tocqueville's heralded tour of America exposed him disproportionately to those whom Professor Friedman describes as "the most prominent, famous lawyers . . . lawyer-statesmen, who argued great cases before great courts, who went into politics, and above all were skilled in the arts of advocacy."[52] As in any other period, this would not have described or included the vast majority of lawyers practicing at that time. And it is certainly true, as more recent scholars have noted, that de Tocqueville's status as a member of the French aristocracy, for whom the far more radical French Revolution had been an unmitigated disaster, caused him to approach his subject with deeply held suspicions about democracy itself.

Nonetheless, de Tocqueville was pleasantly surprised by what he found in ninteenth-century America—and he gave America's lawyers and judges much of the credit. For example, in chapter 8 of *Democracy In America,* titled "What Tempers the Tyranny of the Majority in the United States," de Tocqueville reported to his worldwide audience:

> Visiting Americans and studying their laws, one discovers that the prestige accorded to lawyers and their permitted influence in the government are now the strongest barriers against the faults of democracy. . . .
>
> * * *
>
> Men who have made a special study of the laws and have derived therefrom habits of order, something of taste for formalities, and an instinctive love for a regular concatenation of ideas are naturally strongly opposed to the revolutionary spirit and to the ill-considered passions of democracy.
>
> Study and specialized knowledge of the law give a man a rank apart in society and make of lawyers a somewhat privileged intellectual class. . . [T]hey are the master of a necessary and not widely understood science; they serve as arbiters between the citizens; and the habit of directing the blind passions of the litigants toward the objective gives them a certain scorn for the judgment of the crowd. . . .

* * *

In America there are neither nobles nor men of letters, and the people distrust the wealthy. Therefore the lawyers form the political upper class and the most intellectual section of society. . . .

* * *

If you ask me where the American aristocracy is found, I have no hesitation in answering that it is not among the rich, who have no common life uniting them. It is at the bar or the bench that the American aristocracy is found.[52]

Serving the Common Good and All Those Other Roles

Implicit in de Tocqueville's dated praise,[53] and at the heart of most *positive* critiques and depictions of the legal profession since—the fictional Atticus Finch comes to mind—has been the assumption that lawyers serve and advance the "common good." When lawyers are seen as values-free mouthpieces for amoral clients, that is, as stereotypical hired guns, public respect has plummeted. On the other hand, when lawyers are understood as marching to the beat of a higher drummer than mere self-interest, public respect has followed.

But what is the public or common good, an inquiring mind might ask, in regard to the average contract, real estate closing, commercial or employment dispute, or securities transaction—or even in regard to the typical criminal defense or divorce case? How, if lawyers are to make value judgments about their clients' conduct or intentions, do we decide what—or whose—values, ethics, or morals to apply? And, to use Justice Stone's phrase, can we really avoid becoming "tainted with the morals and manners of the marketplace" in today's highly competitive legal *market?*

These are good questions, of course, that defy simple answers. However, we must be careful in genuflecting to the complexity of contemporary value judgments that we not lose sight of an even larger truth. And the larger truth is this: While there is certainly less "black and white" in how contemporary Americans understand right and wrong, good and evil (or, if you prefer, better and worse), all is not gray either. In other words, as ethicists have warned, we must be careful in acknowledging the complexity of contemporary value judgments not to proceed down the "slippery slope" into complete cynicism and unabashed moral relativism.

In *The Betrayed Profession*, Ambassador Linowitz treats us to a guided historical tour featuring leading lawyers who understood this truth well. Meet, for example, Secretary of State Elihu Root (1845–1937), a "lawyer statesman" who moved freely from successful law practice to periods of celebrated public service, ultimately winning the Nobel Peace Prize in 1912. The sophisticated but plainspoken Root certainly had no problem giving value-based advice. "About half the practice of a decent lawyer," Root once observed, "consists in telling would-be clients that they are damned fools and should stop."[54] In a similar vein, Linowitz laments the loss of an era when a good lawyer would refuse to "undertake the representation of someone he does not trust and whose story he does not believe."[55]

If public respect for the legal profession is to be restored, more attention must be given to this traditional role of the lawyer as "counselor." In the simpler-old-days, when there were fewer laws and those we had were perhaps less "creatively" interpreted, this meant at a minimum "that a good lawyer helped his clients not to evade the law but to obey it."[56] But being a "counselor" also meant—and continues to mean—more than that. It means advising, in circumstances that call for it, not only what the client must do or can get away with doing, but also what the client *should* do. Even if the counsel is ultimately rejected—at which point the lawyer with a conscience may or may not decide to continue the attorney-client relationship—we would do well to emulate the blunt, value-based advice Elihu Root reportedly gave one of his clients: "The law lets you do it, but don't. . . . It's a rotten thing to do."[57]

Closely related to these fundamental ideals—lawyers serving the common good and lawyers providing independent, frequently value-based counsel—is the traditional understanding of the lawyer as "an officer of the court." All three models have implicit or explicit boundaries beyond which the ethical lawyer must refuse to go. Conversely, lawyers who find themselves under fire or even the subjects of criminal prosecution have invariably failed to govern their conduct or counsel under any standard higher than what is perceived at the moment to be in the client's interest. As it turns out, however, having a higher standard than client interest—or, where significant fees are involved, self-interest—is really in every lawyer's best interest.

Another role better lawyers have historically played may surprise those who take for granted the increasingly unforgiving sue-the-bastards approach to dispute resolution. I speak here of the traditional role of more esteemed lawyer/counselors as brokers of reconciliation or, in a word, as peacemakers. That the very concept of lawyers as peacemakers will strike many as impractical or even laughable only underscores the moral vacuum its long-term neglect has created.

In a nutshell, lawyers need to admit to themselves, their clients, and the general public that the benefits of litigation are overrated, with lawyers sometimes being the only real "winners." We need to reflect on the wise counsel of elder lawyer Abraham Lincoln to younger colleagues. "Persuade your neighbors," Lincoln, the renowned *trial lawyer,* wrote, "to compromise whenever you can. Point out to them how the nominal winner is often a real loser—in fees, expenses, and waste of time. As a peacemaker a lawyer has a superior opportunity of being a good man."[58]

What a lovely, if somewhat quaint concept: the lawyer as "a good man"—or to bring the language current, as a good person. But why not, and why not now? Walter Bennett, then a clinical law professor at the University of North Carolina who had absorbed much of the negative data on the contemporary profession, reports "experienc[ing] something close to euphoria" when he discovered, through "oral histories" gathered by his students, that:

> there were lawyers and judges out there who were living lives dedicated to a higher purpose, who loved what they were doing, and who found intellectual richness and creativity in lawyers' work. There were lawyers and judges who had faced loneliness and feelings of powerlessness and had overcome them, sometimes after great struggle and heartache. There were lawyers and judges—very successful, dedicated lawyers and judges—who had learned how to balance their lives at work with their lives as citizens and family members. And, most important, there were lawyers and judges who were proud of being members of the profession, who felt that being a lawyer involved a deep moral commitment, that it was a position not only of prestige but of honor.[59]

The astute reader will note the connection between lawyers and judges who were "living lives dedicated to a higher purpose" and understood lawyering "involved deep moral commitment" and those "who loved what they were doing."

In *The Lawyer's Myth: Reviving Ideals in the Legal Profession,* Professor Bennett reports the "profound effect" these oral histories had on his students, who discovered that "the profession had a heritage that was still alive and cried out to be passed on. . . . "[60] Sensing in these stories "something very close to what Oliver Wendell Holmes called a life of 'passion' in the law," Bennett and his students "studied [their professional experiences] intently . . . for the secrets their lives would yield."[61]

As Professor Bennett summarizes what he and his students discovered:

> Perhaps the most important of those secrets is that passion in one's life's work does not come from a perfection of lawyer's skills or monetary success. It comes from connection with parts of oneself that are rarely recognized in law school or in much of the current lore about being a good lawyer. I found that a passionate life called on something much deeper and greater than anything yielded by the traditional notions of professional success. . . . It had to do with placing one's work as a lawyer, with all the attendant skills and devotion it requires, in the larger context of one's life and one's place in the world.[62]

Two of the "oral histories" collected by Bennett's students are illustrative of this connection between "passion in one's life work" and discovering "the larger context of one's place in the world."

Wade Smith, one of North Carolina's most successful and well-respected lawyers, recollects a day when lawyer jokes would have almost certainly on fallen deaf ears:

> To be a lawyer in the 1960s [when I graduated from law school] was a great honor. . . . The lawyers returned to the small towns in North Carolina. They were president of the PTA; they formed the corporations; they defended people accused of crimes; they headed the United Way campaigns. They really became leaders in their communities. They were very, very much respected in their communities. . . . The lawyers went to the legislature and passed the laws. The lawyers became judges. The lawyers were the governors. Lawyers were an honorable, honest, distinguished group of people. They wanted to make the world better. They were idealists. They struggled to make the world better. . . . They went to law school because it was a way to make the world better.[63]

Although his practice experience was in a smaller town on the other side of the state, the late Sam J. Ervin III, then Chief Judge of the U.S. Court of Appeals for the Fourth Circuit, gave a similar report:

> Lawyers had a much higher standing in the average town or city . . . than they have now. I think they were looked up to as the leaders of the com-

> munity, the people that you would expect to take on civic responsibilities, people who were primarily interested in seeing that justice was being done and who were not primarily interested in seeing how much money they could make.[64]

Judge Ervin went on in the interview, as have many in his generation who remember a brighter professional day, to concede with sadness that "the lawyer has lost a great deal of prestige and respect . . . [and] the profession . . . is not nearly as highly regarded today. . . ."[65] These concessions did not communicate helpless resignation to Professor Bennett or his students, however, and they need not have that effect on us. Rather, consistent with the counsel against unproductive nostalgia for a mythical golden age, we can be properly encouraged that lawyers in recent memory were "passionate" about their work, "were living lives dedicated to a higher purpose," and were well respected by the public they served.

If the bad news is a profession on "the edge of chaos"[66] and "in danger of losing its soul,"[67] the good news is a rich heritage stretching back hundreds of years from which we can draw wisdom and seek contemporary guidance. Historically and even recently, there have been lawyers in a variety of practice contexts—from major city firms to small town solo practitioners—who have understood law as a "high calling," who have balanced the business of law with a commitment to public service, and as a direct consequence of their "ideals," have been held in high public regard.

Rekindling Ideals

Of course, understanding the lessons of the past—the good, the bad, and the ugly—will have little practical effect if they are not actively applied in the present. We can be justifiably proud of what Professor Rhode calls the "broader truth":[68] the fact that "[t]he legal profession is . . . responsible for much that is best in American democratic processes."[69] We can be properly encouraged by de Tocqueville's lofty praise for the role lawyers and judges played in the formation of our democratic republic, and by larger-than-life forbears like Lincoln and Elihu Root. What matters most, however, is that knowledge of this rich heritage motivate us, as individuals and as a profession, to rekindle the ideals that propelled and made these success stories possible.

Although the application of these higher ideals to contemporary practice raises complex questions and will require decades of arduous effort, happily, the ideals themselves can be rather simply stated. First and foremost, we must reaffirm our commitment to serve the "common good;" that is, we must embrace the historical understanding of law as a public service profession. This means more than participation in civic activities primarily as a means to attract new clients or business. Rather, it means that we understand a "calling" to public service as being at the very heart of who we are as a profession and as individual lawyers. Justice Brandeis's exhortation in 1903—warning lawyers "that they were losing public respect because they were also losing their commitment to public service"—is just as true today as it was 100 years ago.

Once we cross this philosophical rubicon—that is, once we affirm law as a calling that transcends client or self-interest—the remaining points logically fall into place. From the basic idea of lawyers striving to serve the common good, it is an easy next step to affirm the traditional understanding of lawyers as "counselors," as "officers of the court," and as "peacemakers." And it is precisely in the rehabilitation and rigorous application of these core ideals and values that our contemporary reform efforts should be grounded. As we have seen, the lawyer as "counselor" will reject the cynical notion that scorns value-based advice. How much better, and more rewarding, to spend a professional lifetime seeking to provide increasingly wise counsel. As an officer of the court, the lawyer will recognize that the boundaries created by an ethical practice are beneficial to both lawyer and client—and are completely nonnegotiable. And understanding that early dispute resolution is often better for the client and for society than full-blown litigation, lawyers who wisely counsel and who govern their conduct as officers of the court will increasingly find themselves in the "blessed" role, once again, of peacemaker.[70]

Can the "dignity and honor" and public respect that have characterized the profession's brighter days be recovered? Can clarified vision and renewed ideals lift us from the "slough of despond" in which much of the profession now finds itself to the more-sustaining and even exhilarating views of the higher peaks?[71] And can lawyers on the brink of what the Japanese call "karoshi" (defined as "death from overwork")[72] discover and cultivate the kind of "passion in the law" Justice Holmes advocated and Professor Bennett and his students serendipitously found in compiling their oral histories?[73]

Yes, yes, and yes, but certainly not without a sustained and concerted effort, and then only if we have the collective nerve for it. Certainly many trends and pressures pull against us and it is not extreme to recognize ours as a profession "in crisis." And yet, if individual lawyers in increasing numbers are spurred to principled, conscientious action—and if law schools, firms, bar organizations, and the courts will support and cooperate, as discussed in chapter 5—the legal profession's best days just might still lie ahead.

Notes

1. MARY ANN GLENDON, A NATION UNDER LAWYERS 3 (1994).
2. ANTHONY T. KRONMAN, THE LOST LAWYER: FAILING IDEALS OF THE LEGAL PROFESSION 1-2 (1993).
3. In addition to practicing law in New York and Washington at various times, Linowitz served as U.S. Ambassador to the Organization of American States under Presidents Johnson and Nixon, negotiated the Panama Canal Treaties under President Carter, and served as general counsel and chairman of the board of Xerox Corporation.
4. *See, e.g.*, SOL M. LINOWITZ (with MARTIN MAYER), THE BETRAYED PROFESSION: LAWYERING AT THE END OF THE TWENTIETH CENTURY (1994).
5. The studies indicating increased lawyer dissatisfaction and dysfunction are reported and discussed in chapter 2.
6. *See, e.g.*, MARC GALANTER, "The Faces of Mistrust: The Image of Lawyers in Public Opinion, Jokes, and Political Discourse," 66 U. CIN. L. REV. 805 (Spring 1998); GARY A. HENGSTLER, "Vox Populi: The Public Perception of Lawyers: ABA Poll," A.B.A.J., Sept. 1993, at 60-65; CHRIS KLEIN, "Poll: Lawyers Not Liked," NAT'L L.J., Aug. 25, 1997, at A6 (Harris poll); RANDALL SAMBORN, "Anti-Lawyer Attitude Up," NAT'L L.J., Aug. 9, 1993, at A1 (*National Law Journal*/West Publishing Co. poll); LAWRENCE SAVELL, "Why Are They Picking On Us?," A.B.A.J., Nov. 1992, at 72.
7. *See, e.g.*, GALANTER, *supra* note 6, at 816-45, citing DAVID L. YAS, "First Thing We Do Is Kill All The Lawyer Jokes," MASS. LAW. WKLY., Oct. 20, 1997 (reporting inter alia that there were at that time at least 3,473 web sites devoted to lawyer jokes).
8. ROGER E. SCHECHTER, "Changing Law Schools to Make Less Nasty Lawyers," 10 GEO. J. LEGAL ETHICS 367 (Winter 1997). Schechter is a Professor of Law at George Washington University.
9. *Id.* at 367-68 (internal footnotes omitted).
10. *Id.* at 394 n.1, citing HENGSTLER, *supra* note 6, at 60. "Scores for other professions ranged from 84 percent favorable for teachers to 60 percent for accountants [before Enron!] to 56 percent for bankers." *Id.*

11. *See* SAMBORN, *supra* note 6, at 20.
12. HENGSTLER, *supra* note 6, at 62.
13. KLEIN, *supra* note 6, at A6.
14. *Id.*
15. DEBORAH L. RHODE, IN THE INTERESTS OF JUSTICE: REFORMING THE LEGAL PROFESSION 1 (2000). Rhode also directs the Keck Center on Legal Ethics and the Legal Profession at Stanford Law School, is a past-president of the Association of American Law Schools and Chair of the ABA Commission on Women in the Profession.
16. *Id.*
17. *Quoted in* SAVELL, *supra* note 6, at 72.
18. *See, e.g.,* ALEXIS DE TOCQUEVILLE, *Democracy in America* (J. P. Mayer ed. Harper & Row 1969) at ____. (1835) GLENDON, *supra* note 1, at 280; Dick Dahl, *The Trouble with Lawyers,* THE BOSTON GLOBE MAGAZINE, Apr. 14, 1996, at 28.
19. WALTER BENNETT, THE LAWYER'S MYTH: REVIVING IDEALS IN THE LEGAL PROFESSION 62(2001)(footnote omitted). *Accord* LAWRENCE W. FRIEDMAN, A HISTORY OF AMERICAN LAW, 2D ED. 96(1985) *and* GALANTER, *supra* note 6, at 810–11.
20. *Quoted in* RHODE, *supra* note 15, at 117.
21. GALANTER, *supra* note 6, at 810–11 (internal footnotes omitted).
22. Although Harvard University established the first university-based law school in 1817, most American lawyers continued to enter the profession through apprenticeships and "reading for the bar" well into the ninteenth century. Uniform standards for law school education, admission to the bar, and discipline of offending practitioners were not firmly established in the United States until the next century, largely through the efforts of the American Bar Association (founded in 1878) and the Association of American Law School (founded in 1900).
23. RHODE, *supra* note 15, at 1, citing AMERICAN LAWYER, *quoted in* MARC GALANTER and THOMAS PALAY, *The Law Firm and the Public Good* 19, 38–39 (Robert A. Katzmann ed., Brookings Institution 1995). On this point, *see also* MARC GALANTER, *Predators and Parasites: Lawyer-Bashing and Civil Justice,* 28 GA. L. REV. 633, 670 (1994).
24. *Quoted in* RHODE, *supra* note 15, at 12.
25. *See* text accompanying note 23, *supra.*
26. MARC GALANTER, *A Nation Under Lost Lawyers: The Legal Profession at the Close of the Twentieth Century,* 100 DICK. L. REV. 549, 552 (Spring 1996), quoting GLENDON, *supra* note 1, at 35, 37.
27. *See* RHODE, *supra* note 15, at 11–12; GALANTER, *supra* note 26, at 549–62.
28. GALANTER, *supra* note 26, at 553.
29. *Quoted in* FRIEDMAN, *supra* note 19, at 578.
30. *Id.* at 648.

31. *Id.* at 572, citing THE MAGNIFICENT SHYSTERS (1947).
32. RHODE, *supra* note 15, at 11, quoting GLENDON, *supra* note 1, at 57.
33. *See* text accompanying notes 23 and 24.
34. RHODE, *supra* note 15, at 12.
35. GALANTER, *supra* note 6, at 811 (notes omitted).
36. FRIEDMAN, *supra* note 19, at 633 (notes omitted).
37. GLENDON, *supra* note 1, at 88.
38. Due to the increased number of licensed lawyers who have gone on "inactive" status with their state and local bars, and/or are working in nonlegal positions, it becomes increasingly difficult to determine who qualifies as a "lawyer," and once that issue is resolved, to identify and accurately count them. The 1992 *World Book Encyclopedia* reported that there were then "over 750,000 lawyers" in the United States, and ABA figures are roughly in accord. Those charged with counting lawyer heads at the ABA, acknowledging the increased complexity of who gets counted, are the author's source for the contemporary number.
39. HARRY T. EDWARDS, "A New Vision for the Legal Profession," 72 N.Y.U. L. REV. 567, 571–72 (Spring 1997)(reprinting Judge Edwards ALI speech).
40. FRIEDMAN, *supra* note 19, at 634.
41. *Id.* at 637–38.
42. GLENDON, *supra* note 1, at 28.
43. ROYANNE C. BAILEY, "Changing Demographics Challenge Lawyers," *Breaking Traditions: Work Alternatives For Lawyers* 13 (Donna M. Killoughey ed., American Bar Association 1993).
44. BENNETT, *supra* note 19, at 93.
45. RHODE, *supra* note 15, at 3.
46. *Id.*
47. CARL T. BOGUS, "The Death of an Honorable Profession," 71 IND. L. J. 911 (Fall 1996).
48. *Id.* at 930.
49. *See* text accompanying notes 18–21.
50. DE TOCQUEVILLE, *supra* note 18 (emphasis added).
51. *Id.*
52. FRIEDMAN, *supra* note 19, at 635.
53. DE TOCQUEVILLE, *supra* note 18.
54. *Quoted in* LINOWITZ, *supra* note 4, at 4.
55. *Id.* at 31.
56. *Id.* at 3.
57. *Id.* at 48.
58. *Id.* at 14.
59. BENNETT, *supra* note 19, at 6.
60. *Id.*

61. *Id.*.
62. *Id.* at 6–7.
63. *Id.* at 35.
64. *Id.* at 35–36.
65. *Id.*
66. *See* text at note 1.
67. *See* text at note 2.
68. *See* text at notes 45–46.
69. *See* text at note 45.
70. In perhaps the best known of the beatitudes, which serve as an introduction to the "Sermon on the Mount," Jesus said, "*Blessed* are the peacemakers: for they shall be called the children of God." See *Matthew* 5:9 (emphasis added).
71. In *Pilgrim's Progress*, English author and preacher John Bunyan (1628–1688) likened life's spiritual journey to a trek that includes periodic entanglement in what he called "the slough of despond." In sharp contrast are life's moments, freed from such entanglements and having made the hard climb to the top, when one enjoys clear vision and brilliant views from life's figurative "peaks."
72. *See* GLENDON, *supra* note 1, at 87; MARA ELEINA CONWAY, "KAROSHI: Is It Sweeping America?" 15 UCLA PAC. BASIN L.J. 353 (1997); TATSUO INOUE, "The Poverty of Rights-Blind Communality: Looking through The Window of Japan," 1993 BRIG. YOUNG L. REV. 517, 532–38.
73. *See* text at notes 61–62.

CHAPTER 2

Troubling Trends: Less Satisfaction, More Dysfunction

"Miserable." That is how a front-page *Los Angeles Times* article described an increasing number of California lawyers in 1995.[1] The next year, 3000 miles away in Boston, "The Misery Factor" was the theme chosen by the Women's Bar Association of Massachusetts for its regularly scheduled meeting.[2] The meandering title of *The Boston Globe Magazine* feature article on the bar meeting captured its essence: "The Trouble with Lawyers: It's Not What You Think. The trouble with lawyers, as many of them are quick to admit, is simple: They're miserable."[3]

Journalists writing articles about lawyers for the popular press are not alone in reaching this conclusion. Harvard Law Professor Mary Ann Glendon, in her insightful 1994 survey of the profession, asks plaintively, "Why are so many lawyers so sad?"[4] In *The Betrayed Profession: Lawyering at the End of the Twentieth Century*, Ambassador Sol M. Linowitz announces simply, "I write about an unhappy profession."[5] And lawyer-turned-psychotherapist Benjamin Sells, who left a prestigious Chicago law practice to treat lawyers in various stages of psychological and emotional distress, concludes "Lawyers in today's world are lonely, painfully lonely."[6]

Strong, unequivocal words: miserable, so sad, unhappy profession, painfully lonely. Not words, to be sure, that yet apply to a majority of the nation's lawyers, who continue to report that they are at least somewhat satisfied with their chosen profession,[7] but words that point nonetheless to troubling trends affecting a substantial minority.

In *The Soul of the Law: Understanding Lawyers and Law*, Dr. Benjamin Sells seeks to explain "the lingering feeling of emptiness despite material success"[8] many contemporary lawyers experience. Assuming heightened levels of distress and dysfunction as a given, Sells notes:

> Report after report tells us that lawyers experience psychological unrest at much higher levels than non-lawyers. A survey of 105 occupations showed lawyers first on the list in experiencing depression; another study reports that fully *one-third* of all attorneys suffer from either depression, alcohol or drug abuse . . . ; anxiety and obsessive behavior afflict a disproportionately large number of lawyers, sometimes to the point of incapacitation; many lawyers report strong feelings of isolation and social alienation; and upwards of sixty percent of lawyers say they would not recommend the law as a career to their own children.[9]

The "survey of 105 occupations" to which Dr. Sells refers was conducted in 1990 by researchers affiliated with Johns Hopkins University (and actually covered *104* occupations).[10] The purpose of the study was to determine the prevalence of "major depressive disorder" (MDD), from which 3 to 5 percent of the general public is believed to suffer, in each of the targeted occupations.[11]

What the Johns Hopkins researchers found, and has since been corroborated by other studies and surveys, is that major depression afflicts a significantly higher than average percentage of lawyers. In fact, law was one of only five occupations in the Johns Hopkins study in which the occurrence of MDD exceeded 10 percent—and lawyers topped even this list, suffering from major depression "at a rate 3.6 times higher than non-lawyers who shared their same sociodemographic traits."[12] Findings such as these have led commentators to pronounce law an "unhealthy"[13] and "high-risk"[14] vocation, and another to conclude that "the professional and personal well-being of lawyers is in serious jeopardy."[15]

Troubling Trends: Surveys and Studies

Although the collective message of recent bar surveys and academic studies can only be characterized as "troubling," that is not the whole story either. If the glass is one-third or even one-half empty, it is also still at least half-full. Depending on which surveys are deemed most credible, Stanford Law Professor Deborah L. Rhode is probably correct that "[w]hen asked directly about their current position, the vast majority of surveyed lawyers express satisfaction."[16]

It is certainly true that along with the more alarming findings—for example, the finding in a 1989 statewide survey that 11 percent of North Carolina lawyers had considered suicide at least once a month during the preceding year[17]—there also have been more encouraging results from time to time. A 1995 ABA survey of "young lawyers," defined as lawyers under 36 *or* in practice less than three years, found, for example, that "about three-quarters were somewhat or very satisfied with their current positions."[18] In 2000, in a study titled "The Pulse of the Profession" ("the ABA Pulse Study"), the ABA extended its market research to all segments of the practicing bar—and reached mixed, but generally positive, conclusions.[19] On the other hand, even the more optimistic ABA conceded in its 2000 report that "concerned" was "the word that best sum[med] up the overall attitudinal 'pulse' of the legal profession" at that time.[20]

The 2000 ABA Pulse Study—based on 14 focus groups conducted in cities located in three different regions (Chicago, Illinois; Sacramento, California; and Birmingham, Alabama), including lawyers from all experience levels and firm sizes—found lawyers feeling "pretty good" about their vocations and generally appreciative of certain professional benefits.[22] Specifically, lawyers in the focus groups reported that they enjoy: intellectual challenge, an interesting variety in their work, having their opinions valued and "the tools to affect change" at their disposal, being part of "an elite group of professionals," and making "good money."[21] But again, along with the positive and hopeful, the specific "concerns" noted in the report were by no means insignificant.

Holding "little doubt [that] the legal profession is at an important crossroads,"[23] the lawyers who participated in the ABA 2000 focus groups were "concerned" about the following "real-life trends":[24]

- Financial pressures that are transforming law from a profession to a business;
- Clients becoming increasingly demanding;
- A lack of mentoring the next generation of attorneys;
- The increasingly central (and double-edged) role of technology;
- A growing public distrust and disrespect for the legal profession; and
- An erosion of professional courtesy and sense of community.[25]

Although certainly not as alarming as Dr. Benjamin Sells's comparison of "the Law" to a man "suffering from a lack of oxygen,"[26] the ABA's juxtaposition of most lawyers feeling "pretty good" about their professional lives with widespread "concern" about these "real-life trends" might strike the more cynical reader as fodder for a good news/bad news joke.

There is nothing inherently wrong about focusing on these "half-full" elements and, in fact, excessive focus on the negative without "the rest of the story" can be both misleading and debilitating. However, neither can we escape the troubling trends in almost two decades of surveys and studies. And with regard to lawyer satisfaction, the trends have clearly been in the wrong direction.

As it turns out, the most comprehensive data on lawyer career satisfaction/dissatisfaction comes from three national surveys conducted by the ABA: companion surveys conducted in 1984 and 1990, and the previously noted survey of "young lawyers" conducted in 1995. The first surveyed more than 3,000 lawyers (including both ABA members and nonmembers) in what was then described as "the first in-depth survey of the legal profession in order to accurately study the state of the profession and determine the extent of career dissatisfaction."[27] The second, conducted in 1990, surveyed the lawyers who responded in 1984 a second time, as well as 1,000 lawyers who had since been admitted to practice.

What the 1984 and 1990 ABA surveys found, in a nutshell, was a 20-percent drop—during those six years alone—in the number of lawyers describing themselves as "very satisfied."[28] During the same period, the percentage of those describing themselves as "dissatisfied" or "very dissatisfied" rose sharply. As the ABA matter-of-factly reported its 1990 findings:

> In the past six years, the extent of lawyer dissatisfaction has increased throughout the profession. It is now reported in significant numbers by lawyers in all positions—partners as well as junior associates. It is now present in significant numbers in firms of all sizes, not just the largest and the smallest firms.[29]

Although Professor Rhode's observation that a majority of surveyed lawyers "express satisfaction" holds for the 1984 and 1990 ABA surveys, the rest of the story is unavoidably troubling: for example, 22 percent of all male partners and 43 percent of all female partners reporting dissatisfaction, and more than a doubling of lawyers who described themselves as "very dissatisfied."[30]

Certainly those conducting the surveys recognized the startling implications of their findings, as evidenced by the national conference convened by the ABA in April 1991 under the rather unwieldy title, "At the Breaking Point: The Emerging Crisis in the Quality of Lawyers' Health and Lives, and Its Impact on Law Firms and Client Services." Having considered the survey results and the conference presentations, the conference report simply and soberly concluded:

> There is a growing trend in the legal profession which, left unchecked, threatens the well-being of all lawyers and firms in every part of the country.[31]

Although the 1995 ABA survey found three-quarters of the "young lawyers" at least somewhat satisfied, it did little to allay concerns about a growing, disenchanted minority.

As Patrick J. Schiltz, then an Associate Professor of Law at Notre Dame Law School analyzes it, there was an even darker side to the ABA survey results:

> Even though the attorneys surveyed in 1995 had just started their legal careers, over 27 percent were already "somewhat" or "very" dissatisfied with the practice of law; only about one in five was "very" satisfied. Almost one-third of the young lawyers said that they would "strongly" consider leaving their current position in the next two years, and almost another third said that they "might" consider doing so.[32]

However it is analyzed, the collective teaching of the ABA surveys in 1984, 1990, and 1995, and the Pulse Study in 2000, is this: A majority of lawyers remain at least somewhat satisfied with what we will call "LawyerLife." On the other hand, a minority, which began to grow in the 1980s and may or may not have plateaued, has become at least somewhat dissatisfied. And a not insignificant number of the dissatisfied—those who regularly consider killing themselves, for example—are truly miserable.

A number of less-comprehensive surveys bear out these conclusions. Surveys of the Maryland, North Carolina, New Jersey, and California bars conducted between 1988 and 1992, and surveys of University of Michigan Law School graduates conducted between 1976 and 1996, generally support the ABA findings. On the other hand, surveys of the graduates of the three Minnesota law schools, members of the New York Bar Association, and Chicago lawyers, conducted between 1987 and 1995, produced more-favorable results.

In 1988, the Maryland State Bar Association's "Committee on Law Practice Quality" conducted more than 1,000 telephone interviews with lawyers from various locations and law-firm sizes, asking each interviewee 142 questions. Because it was something of a pioneer finding at that time, those conducting the survey were surprised to discover that "almost a third of the respondents were not sure they wanted to keep on practicing law."[33] Reflecting on their findings, the Committee reported that:

> the personal lives of all attorneys seem to be adversely affected by the demands on their professional lives. Sixty-nine percent of the lawyers fell into the range of [only] somewhat satisfied to completely dissatisfied with the way their work lives mesh with their personal, family, social and civic lives, and 59 percent foresaw that there would be no change in their future work relationships.[34]

In 1989, in response to anecdotal evidence of lawyer discontent (including eight lawyer suicides in Charlotte during a seven-year period), the North Carolina Bar Association created a Quality of Life Task Force.[35] Following a statewide survey at least as comprehensive as its Maryland counterpart, the 1991 task force report concluded that there was "a severe level of dissatisfaction with law practice among some attorneys and lost dreams and idealism among many others."[36] The North Carolina survey also found:

- Twenty-four percent of North Carolina's lawyers would not become lawyers if they could make the decision again;
- Only 54 percent wished to remain in law practice for the remainder of their careers;
- More than 24 percent reported symptoms of depression "at least three times per month during the past year," with 11 percent reporting they had considered suicide at least once a month during the same year; and
- Forty-three percent agreed the demands of work did allow them "to have enough time for life outside of work."[37]

At about the same time the North Carolina lawyers were being polled, the New Jersey State Bar Association was interviewing 375 of its members. The New Jersey findings were broadly consistent with those in North Carolina:

- Twenty-five percent of the New Jersey lawyers were "very satisfied" with their professional life, 44 percent "reasonably" satisfied, 20 percent "somewhat dissatisfied", and 3 percent "very dissatisfied";
- Ninteen percent were "somewhat dissatisfied" with their opportunities to engage in community activities; [and] 20 percent were "somewhat dissatisfied" with the opportunities to "contribute to society";
- Forty-one percent planned to change careers before retirement, 13 percent within the next two years; and
- Eighty-two percent were experiencing "excessive or unhealthy stress in their current life."[38]

We began this chapter by quoting a 1995 *Los Angeles Times* article describing a significant portion of California's lawyers as "miserable." The polls certainly appear to bear out this unhappy assessment, including a 1992 California Bar Association survey which found that *70 percent* "would choose another career if they had the opportunity and . . . *75 percent* would not want their children to become lawyers."[39] Two years later, a survey conducted by the RAND Institute for Civil Justice found California lawyers "profoundly pessimistic" about their careers, although the percentage who would choose another profession if they could had fallen to around 50 percent.[40] On the other hand, this "improvement" might partly be due to the sharp rise in California lawyers who had gone on "inactive status with the State Bar"—around 25 percent in 1995, up from 10 percent in 1980.[41]

Although not as miserable as their California counterparts, graduates of the University of Michigan Law School—who are dispersed nationally—have reported comparable decreases in professional satisfaction in recent years. The Michigan Law School surveys, which since 1976 have asked former students five years after graduation to report on career satisfaction/dissatisfaction, also allow us to observe how attitudes of a relatively homogenous group of lawyers have developed over time.

Professor Patrick Schiltz, whose lead article in a 1999 issue of the *Vanderbilt Law Review,* "On Being a Happy, Healthy, and Ethical Member of an Unhappy, Unhealthy, and Unethical Profession,"[42] delighted some and annoyed others, was clearly correct in his analysis of the Michigan Law School surveys. Schiltz explains:

> For almost thirty years, the University of Michigan Law School has been surveying its former students five years after they graduate. The last survey for which results have been reported was conducted in 1996. Given the stellar reputation of their alma mater, Michigan graduates would presumably have more employment options available than graduates of most other law schools and thus would presumably be among the most satisfied practitioners in America. Yet the annual surveys have discovered surprisingly low levels of career satisfaction in general and a marked decline in career satisfaction over time, at least for lawyers in private practice.
>
> For example, the percentage of graduates working as solo practitioners or in firms of fifty or fewer lawyers who were "quite satisfied" with their careers five years after graduation fell from 45 percent for members of the classes of 1976 and 1977 (and from a high of 52 percent for members of the classes of 1980 and 1981) to 37 percent for members of the classes of 1990 and 1991. The percentage of graduates working in firms of 51 or more lawyers who were "quite satisfied" with their careers fell from 53 percent for members of the classes of 1976 and 1977 (and from a high of 54 percent for the classes of 1978 and 1979) to 30 percent for members of the classes of 1990 and 1991. In the rather understated words of the Michigan Law School survey, "this picture is gloomy."[43]

On the other hand, not every survey on the career satisfaction of lawyers has yielded such negative results, and there are those who disagree that growing lawyer unhappiness is a significant problem. In a 1987 survey of graduates of three Minnesota law schools, for example, 94 percent of the respondents reported that they were either "satisfied" or "very satisfied" with their current jobs.[44] A 1994 survey of members of the New York bar "found generally high levels of career satisfaction among lawyers."[45] And in a 1995 survey, 84 percent of Chicago lawyers reported that they were either "very satisfied" (45 percent) or "satisfied" (39 percent), about 10 percent were neutral, and only 7 percent were either "dissatisfied" (5 percent) or "very dissatisfied" (2 percent).[46] And the 1988 results notwithstanding,[47] in a 1998 survey of Maryland State Bar Association members, 74 percent of the respondents described the quality of their professional life as "good" or "very good," and 90 percent reported that they were able to balance work and family "some or all of the time."[48]

A minority of commentators, noting these surveys and questioning the reliability or interpretation of those appearing to produce less-favorable results, continue to challenge what sociologist Kathleen E. Hull has called "the myth of lawyers' misery."[49] Like Hull, they argue that "the most valid, well-designed research has produced little if any support for the notion that lawyers are unhappy in their work."[50] They point specifically to low response rates and/or unscientific research techniques, either of which might skew the results because "there is no way to know for sure whether disgruntled lawyers were disproportionately willing to participate."[51]

If a balanced understanding of the surveys and studies on lawyer satisfaction/dissatisfaction is the goal, we must ignore neither the majority of lawyers who continue to express satisfaction *nor* the minority —however large or small it is—who are clearly and undeniably unhappy. Professor Deborah Rhode strikes this balance when, immediately after acknowledging that "the vast majority of surveyed lawyers express satisfaction," she continues:

> Yet . . . other evidence paints a gloomier picture. A majority of lawyers report that they would choose another career if they had the decision to make over, and three-quarters would not want their children to become lawyers. Only one-fifth of attorneys feel that the law has lived up to their expectations in contributing to the social good. Symptoms of professional malaise are also apparent in health-related difficulties. An estimated one-third of American attorneys suffer from depression or from alcohol or drug addiction, a rate that is two to three times higher than in the public generally.[52]

And, finally, there is the growing body of anecdotal evidence. Every lawyer and every judge knows lawyers who are in various stages of distress, who are working too hard or drinking too much, whose family lives are unraveling, or who increasingly find themselves on a depressing "treadmill" with little hope of rekindling professional enthusiasm. As described in *Law v. Life*, the reaction to Walt Bachman's resignation as a firm partner "to write, teach, and pursue a more service-oriented path"[53] is anecdotal, but nonetheless rich in instructional value. Bachman, who holds law degrees from Oxford and Stanford Universities and is a former Rhodes Scholar, writes:

> Time and again, lawyers at the pinnacle of their careers telephoned me or came into my office (usually closing the door discreetly behind them so as not to be overheard) to reveal their secret aspirations for escaping from their lives in the law. The recurrent themes of these emotion-laden conversations were disillusionment, lack of satisfaction, and a sense of hand-wringing dismay over the direction the legal profession had taken. Lawyers making up to a third of a million dollars expressed their vision of chucking it all to run a bait shop in northern Minnesota, teach inner-city kids, or manage a symphony orchestra. Some told me they were actively squirreling away money to finance their fantasies.[54]

Although Bachman recognized that many of the lawyers who affirmed his decision to leave practice would *not* follow in his footsteps, the fact that so many were empathetic itself speaks volumes.

Devil in the Details

As the old saw goes, cautioning against over-generalization, "The devil is in the details." This is certainly true of the details—which draw a fairly consistent and coherent picture—in the surveys and studies on lawyer satisfaction.

First, there are the consistent responses to more-specific questions. Moving beyond subjective self-assessment of professional "satisfaction," lawyers in diverse states and from a wide range of practices have been asked questions like: If you had it to do over, would you become a lawyer? Do you plan to remain in the practice of law until retirement? Would you want your children to become lawyers? The reported answers to these questions are not particularly encouraging.

As noted, somewhere between 50 and 70 percent of California lawyers responded in the early 1990s that they "would choose another career if they had an opportunity"—and that was in addition to the 25 percent who had already become "inactive."[55] In 1989, 24 percent of North Carolina lawyers reported that they "would not become lawyers if they could make the decision again" and "only 54 percent wished to remain in law practice for the remainder of their careers."[56] Around the same time, 41 percent of New Jersey lawyers were reporting that they "planned to change careers before retirement, 13 percent within the next two years."[57] And, a year or two earlier, the Maryland State Bar Association had been surprised to learn that "almost a third of the respondents [to a survey by its "Committee on Law Practice Quality"] were not sure they wanted to keep on practicing law."[58]

What the devil in these details about LawyerLife shows is a high degree of disenchantment—or, in the Maryland results, ambivalence—about the practice of law *by practicing lawyers*. And, of course, this conclusion is confirmed in spades by the troubling percentage of lawyers who would *not* recommend that their own children follow in their professional footsteps: "upwards of 60 percent," according to Dr. Benjamin Sells,[59] and "three-quarters," according to Professor Deborah Rhode.[60]

Reports of excessive "stress," like self-assessed levels of professional satisfaction, are highly subjective. And, of course, what one person finds stressful, dissatisfying, or otherwise unpleasant may strike another as tolerable or even enjoyable. This is true, in part, as someone once put it, because "frustration is a function of expectation."

This is not to suggest that self-reports of dissatisfaction or excessive stress are unreliable or unimportant. Much to the contrary, the fact that between one-third and over three-fourths of practicing lawyers report excessive or unhealthy stress—82 percent in the New Jersey survey[61]—is profoundly troubling. Whatever the numbers in a particular survey, state, or local bar, two additional factors confirm the professionwide need for "stress management." First, there is the growing body of anecdotal evidence, some of which has been reported in the popular or legal press, and much more that is known only within a smaller circle. And more significantly, there is the alarming increase in alcohol and drug abuse, clinical depression, and even suicide—all objectively verifiable manifestations of dissatisfaction, stress, and so forth—among lawyers "from sea to shining sea."

Howard J. Levitan, who calls himself "a recovering lawyer,"[62] is an anecdotal example. Levitan was a partner in a Boston firm with annual income over $300,000 when he resigned and moved to Newcastle, Maine, to become an innkeeper. Although he remains complimentary and even upbeat about his former colleagues—"wonderful firm, with wonderful people"[63]—he decided to leave it all behind when the dark side of "success" yielded migraine headaches, high blood pressure, and intolerable stress.[64]

Elizabeth Brodersen came to a similar conclusion working for a corporate law firm in San Francisco. A graduate of Columbia University Law School, she realized in her mid-30s that the pressure and long hours were making her ill. Although she had enjoyed and done well in law school, once her student loans were paid, Brodersen left law practice to become publications director for the American Conservatory Theater, also in San Francisco. Although her salary was a fourth of what she made practicing law, Brodersen decided her own health required rejection of the Faustian bargain of money for misery.[65]

David A. Deakin reached the same conclusion after a summer clerkship with a large firm where 2,000 annual billable hours "was really just a threshold expectation."[66] Following graduation from Harvard Law School, Deakin—who described work he had been given at the firm as "sort of soul destroying"[67]—decided to become a much lower-paid prosecutor instead.[68] For Levitan, Brodersen, Deakin, and a growing number of others, the benefit of a healthier, more balanced life is becoming *the* determining factor in making career decisions.

Unfortunately, there are many more lawyers who are responding to professional unhappiness and stress in less healthy ways. Some, like the Energizer bunny, just try to keep going and going, unable or unwilling to slow down enough to consider early warning signals. Others slip into the excessive use of alcohol or self-medicate with illegal drugs.

The National Institute on Alcohol and Alcohol Abuse estimates that approximately 10 percent of the adult population in the United States are either alcoholics or are otherwise chemically dependent. Based on studies and surveys—and the high percentage of disciplinary proceedings in which alcohol or drug abuse play a significant part—experts estimate that "[a]bout a fifth of lawyers have a substance abuse problem, twice the rate of Americans generally."[69]

Reflecting on the data available in 1996, several psychologists observed in a scholarly article that "[p]sychological distress and alcoholism do not recognize socioeconomic or professional boundaries"[70] and that "alcohol-related problems remain at all points in lawyers [sic] careers."[71] Lawyer Assistance Programs (LAPs) around the country, often working hand-in-hand with bar disciplinary committees, confirm this scholarly assessment. Indeed, as Dr. Benjamin Sells has written, "[s]ome states report that substance abuse is a factor in up to 75 percent of all disciplinary complaints involving lawyers."[72]

As those who have experienced it are quick to testify, depression can be at least as debilitating as alcohol or drug abuse. And again, the research and survey data, although incomplete, "suggest that the professional and the personal well-being of [many] lawyers is in serious jeopardy."[73]

The 1990 Johns Hopkins study,[74] in which lawyers were found to be suffering with major depressive disorder (MDD) at the highest rate of any of the 104 occupations and professions studied, remains the most exhaustive research on the subject. As noted previously, "[l]awyers topped the list, suffering MDD at a rate 3.6 times higher than non-lawyers who share their same sociodemographic traits."[75]

Although this is the only major study comparing depression in different occupations and professions, the results are consistent with other studies and surveys focused solely on lawyers. In the North Carolina survey conducted sometime between creation of the Quality of Life Task Force in 1989 and publication of its Report in 1991,[76] "[m]ore than 24 percent reported symptoms of depression 'at least three times per month during the past year,' with 11 percent reporting they had considered suicide at least once a month during the same year."[77] Research conducted several years earlier in Arizona and Washington found "one-third of all lawyers [in those states] suffering from either clinical depression or substance abuse, both at twice the general prevalence rates for these disorders."[78]

In 1996, analyzing this and other research for the *Journal of Law and Health*, psychologists Connie J. A. Beck, Bruce D. Sales, and G. Andrew H. Benjamin concluded:

> The data and analyses . . . manifest a highly alarming fact: a significant percentage of practicing lawyers are experiencing a variety of significant psychological distress symptoms well beyond that expected of the general population.[79]

Although that conclusion will not surprise those familiar with the surveys and research reviewed in this chapter, it does confirm the nature and extent of the psychological distress altogether too many contemporary lawyers are facing.

But Do Not Despair

If the goal is a healthy, vibrant bar, we do nothing to advance the ball by denying the unavoidable teachings of this research. The first step toward any potentially effective solution is to understand the nature and extent of the problem. And, as the various twelve-step programs demonstrate, the first move toward healing—which is often the most difficult—is to acknowledge there *is* a problem.

When it comes to the professional satisfaction and health of many of the nation's lawyers, there is clearly "a problem." The trends are troubling, and they have been moving in the wrong direction for at least two decades. A sizeable minority of our sisters and brothers at the bar are dissatisfied with LawyerLife. A significant number are reportedly or apparently miserable. Increasing percentages have fallen into alcohol or drug abuse, clinical depression, or both. And an overwhelming majority of lawyers feel poorly enough about the legal profession that they would not recommend it to their own children.

And yet, that is not the whole story either. We do have deep roots in a rich heritage from which we can draw strength and inspiration. The traditional ideals affirmed in chapter 1 are ideas with positive and hopeful consequences. Indeed, the very fact that an increasing number of lawyers and law professors realize the profession is "in crisis" is itself cause for encouragement.

Increased awareness has already produced some impressive results. Bar leaders, from ABA presidents to leaders of state and local bars around the country, have placed greater emphasis on quality of life and "professionalism" concerns. Many bars have significantly increased time and resources dedicated to lawyer assistance programs. Books, articles, and CLE programs continue to raise awareness of the challenges we face as a profession and as individual practitioners. And a virtual cottage industry of helping professionals has arisen, some of whom are former lawyers who have successfully struggled with these very problems themselves.

Those who need the free and confidential services of a lawyer assistance program (LAP) should contact their state or local bar. The ABA Lawyer Assistance Foundation (formerly Commission on Impaired Attorneys) also maintains a lengthy list of lawyer assistance programs, contacts, and related information. Their contact information:

ABA Lawyer Assistance Foundation
541 N. Fairbanks Court, 14th Floor
Chicago, IL 60611-3314
(312) 988-5359

The Nelson Mullins Riley & Scarborough Center on Professionalism at the University of South Carolina School of Law is another valuable resource. Initiated in 1999 with a $1-million gift from the law firm after which it is named, the center's web site includes a broad list of resources germane to "professionalism" (defined to include quality/

balance-of-life issues)—including professors addressing these issues at hundreds of law schools in all parts of the country. Contact information:

Professor Robert M. Wilcox, Director
NMR&S Center on Professionalism
University of South Carolina School of Law
701 S. Main Street
Columbia, SC 29208
(803) 777-6112
e-mail: robbie@law.law.sc.edu
web site: http://professionalism.law.sc.edu

And finally, there is the growing cadre of lawyers who have found professional satisfaction and balance—often following profound personal struggles and problems—and of helping professionals who offer services specifically designed for those who are still struggling. Some, like lawyer-turned-psychotherapist Benjamin Sells, have developed national reputations. Many more, providing services ranging from career counseling to personalized help with substance abuse, "burnout," or depression, are known only regionally or locally. Collectively, however, their growing numbers and sophistication are reasonable grounds for encouragement.

Steven Keeva, Assistant Managing Editor of the *ABA Journal*, brings an interesting variety of "overcomer lawyers" and helping professionals to our attention in his articles, and in his insightful book, *Transforming Practices: Finding Joy and Satisfaction in the Legal Life*.[80] Some of Keeva's articles, which like his book highlight individual lawyers who *have* found balance and satisfaction in life and in law, are also posted on his web site: http://www.transformingpractices.com.

Keeva introduces us, for example, to John McShane, John McQuiston II, Arnie Herz, Brenda Fingold, and Rick Halpert. While not every one of these lawyers has passed through the darker professional valleys, each appears to be successfully pursuing what Keeva calls "joy and satisfaction in the legal life."[81] After absorbing so much bad news, brief mention of these happier, more hopeful stories should remind us—as we need to be reminded again and again—that there is much that remains positive and praiseworthy in the contemporary practice of law.

Once a raging alcoholic about to be disbarred and "on the brink of suicide," Texas lawyer John McShane "dispatched his demons and dedicated himself to finding fulfillment in the law."[82] McShane, who turned 60 around the turn of the new millennium, recollects a time when one of his clients quietly passed a note to a federal judge claiming that his lawyer was too drunk to represent him. Recalling the judge examining him on the witness stand and eventually allowing the proceeding to continue, McShane "jokes that he's probably the only lawyer in Texas who's been found sober by a federal judge."[83]

That was in the mid-1970s. Since then John McShane has collected a number of what he calls "merit badges."[84] He co-founded "Lawyers Concerned for Lawyers" to help impaired colleagues; his law practice has grown both in depth and breadth; and "in an extraordinary reversal of fortune, he was elected chairman of the State Bar District Six Grievance Committee, the very body that had sought his disbarment years earlier."[85] McShane has also been extraordinarily generous in sharing his "story" with lawyers and law students across the country. Professor Bruce Winnick of the University of Miami School of Law, who invited him to address that student body, describes McShane as "a spellbinding speaker with an important message for all law students and lawyers."

As John McShane and others tell it, his transformation from the brink of personal and professional disaster to a successful, balanced life and law practice is "equal parts emotional, intellectual, and spiritual."[86] Today he disciplines himself daily to slow down and "smell the flowers." Actually, he does not use that expression; he prefers an Italian one: "la dolce far siente," which translates "the sweet doing of nothing."[87] He has also developed a "holistic" or "healing approach" to law and life, which encompasses everything from "snuggling with [his] grandson" to spending late nights empathizing with Texas oil magnate T. Boone Pickens, a client who was then going through a bitter and painful divorce. "I now mention the divorce," Pickens wrote in his autobiography, "and I say that the one positive thing that came out of it was a great friendship with John McShane."[88]

For John McQuiston II, a busy commercial litigator in Memphis, Tennessee, the turning point came as a result of his father's death in 1991. An only child who had lost his mother years earlier and who had been particularly close to this father, he found himself pouring out his heart to an Episcopal priest, a close family friend, after the funeral.[89] Why are we here? What is the relationship of all this work, successful or not, to the real meaning of life? Indeed, *is* there any transcendent meaning? Or questions to that effect.

The priest recommended an unlikely source in response to McQuiston's probing questions: the *Rule of St. Benedict*, a classic text that has governed the daily lives of Benedictine monks since it was authored by Benedict himself in the Sixth Century. McQuiston liked what he read, and immediately saw the relevance of these ancient teachings to the increasing need in his own life for balance and renewed purpose. In 1996, after first rewriting the Rule for personal use, he published *Always We Begin Again: The Benedictine Way of Living*. "Being a lawyer, I wanted to call it *The Rule of St. Benedict Restated*," McQuiston quips, "but the publisher didn't go for that."[90]

What particularly struck John McQuiston about the "Benedictine Way" was the wisdom of its balance not only of the temporal and the spiritual, "but also the balancing of one's inner and outer selves."[91] McQuiston reports not only spiritual discoveries, however. He also advises that "his practice is more enjoyable than ever"; that overcommitment and his "stress level" are way down; and that feeling more at peace with himself on a personal level "has made [him] more relaxed and flexible with clients."[92] According to Steven Keeva, McQuiston has also become "more willing to bring 'a broad range of values' to his law practice"; to give "advice and . . . recommendations about what clients should or shouldn't do much more readily than before"; to help clients "see their cases from outside the narrow perspective of law"; and even to question "whether litigation is the way to go."[93]

Fortunately, it does not always take a personal crisis to bring lawyers into a healthy, life-sustaining balance. Arnie Herz, who traveled to Europe and spent two years in India studying yoga and meditation before he attended law school, was considered one of New York's most gifted mediators before he turned 40.[94] As one happy lawyer put it after successful mediation of a case that would "never settle," Herz "used his perceptions about human nature to break down everybody's walls and the barriers that separated the two clients."[95] In a word, Arnie Herz has become a highly skilled peacemaker.

By all reports, Herz' clients—which "include a wide variety of businesses, Internet and other high-tech companies, and even a successful actress, Phylicia Rashad, late of *The Cosby Show*"[96]—are equally pleased with his focus and balance. On the one hand, Herz spends his 45-minute morning commute in quiet meditation and reflection and tries continually to help his clients calmly consider what is *really* in their best interest. On the other hand, he is described both by clients and opposing counsel as a smart, "tough negotiator" who "leave[s] no stone unturned."[97]

Brenda Fingold, a partner in a Boston firm with more than 350 lawyers, is another who has looked east—in her case, to the practice of "mindfulness"—to reduce stress and increase satisfaction in the contemporary practice. The idea is not a novel one; researchers at the Stress Reduction Clinic of the University of Massachusetts Medical Center have used "mindfulness" practices, which are rooted in the Buddhist tradition, "to reduce stress and enhance health and well being" for more than 20 years.[98] The Nyingma Institute in Berkeley, California, which also uses practices from the mindfulness tradition in its one-day stress-reduction courses for lawyers, has had similar success.[99]

"When I'm meditating regularly and focusing on being mindful," Fingold reports, "I'm more productive and creative in my work. I also deal more effectively with daily challenges."[100] Realizing the benefits she was gleaning personally, Fingold used her role as partner in charge of training and professional development to make hers "the first law firm in the country to offer a mindfulness-based stress-reduction course for its lawyers."[101] Since its creation in the 1990s, a substantial number of the partners and associates have completed the course, which involves a two-hour session once a week for eight weeks.[102]

Rick Halpert and his partners in Kalamazoo, Michigan have found satisfaction in their personal injuries practice not through spiritual or stress-reduction exercises, but through going the extra mile with their clients. As Keeva puts it, "The lawyers aren't saints, nor do they live monastic lives, but they have built a highly successful law firm on a solid foundation of caring, uncommon attentiveness to clients' needs, and advocacy that serves the client in a broad and holistic way."[103]

Halpert's firm even developed a mission statement—"to improve clients' lives physically, psychologically, emotionally, and financially"[104]—to keep itself on a distinctively different course. At various times this has included driving clients without family or friends to distant hospitals, establishing a summer camp for burn victims, returning to the home of a former client each Christmas, dressed as Santa Claus and bearing gifts for his young daughters, paying for parents of badly injured children to travel to participate in life-changing support groups, and countless hours of just listening and empathizing.[105]

"When you're emotionally intimate with a person going through a terrible time and you can make a difference, there's incredible joy in that," says Halpert.[106] And if we need further proof that Halpert and his partners are on to something significant, consider this unlikely fact for a highly successful *personal injuries* firm: Doctors and nurses are a significant source of their new clients, recommending the firm primarily "because of the *nonmonetary* benefits it offers." These health professionals recommend the firm because, like themselves, they see Halpert and his partners as being in the healing business.

David Link, Dean Emeritus of the University of Notre Dame Law School, has done extensive research on the historical role of lawyers as "healers," and is convinced that the earliest lawyers routinely performed this kinder and gentler function. "What has happened in recent years," Link explains, "is that legal ethics have become adversarial ethics."[107] Dean Link "believes it is time for lawyers to reclaim their role as healers," as does Rob Lehman, president of the Fetzer Institute in western Michigan.[108]

A lawyer himself, Rob Lehman recalls a time similar to what Professor Bennett discovered in his "oral histories."[109] "I grew up in a town of 3,000 where we had two doctors and two lawyers," Lehman remembers. "And I always thought of the lawyer as somewhat similar to the doctor. You went to the lawyer for a problem, and that lawyer would really help."[110] Lehman continues:

> You really looked to the lawyer in town as someone of enormous stature and respect, and that person could help you through life's problems and crises more than just a technical way. And I think there is almost an implicit, almost inchoate healing character to the lawyer in our tradition, certainly in the idea of the wise counselor and listening person.[111]

To help lawyers "unpack their history" and "to explore just what it means to be a lawyer-healer," the Fetzer Institute has developed a "Healing and the Law Project."[112] This includes "a nationwide search for stories that demonstrate lawyers' capacity for healing," an effort directed by Dean Link.[113] Those with stories to contribute, or who would like more information on how a healing component can be incorporated in contemporary law practice, should contact:

Fetzer Institute
9292 West KL Avenue
Kalamazoo, MI 49009
(616) 375-2000
e-mail: info@fetzer.org

George W. Kaufman is another who has devoted the latter part of his career to helping lawyers find personal and professional satisfaction. A 1962 graduate of Yale Law School with a distinguished 35-year career under his belt, Kaufman began to offer workshops for unhappy or stressed-out lawyers in the mid-1990s. Encouraged by the response, he developed the workshop materials into a helpful book, *The Lawyer's Guide to Balancing Life and Work: Taking the Stress Out of Success*, published by the ABA in 1999. To schedule a workshop, or for more information, contact:

George W. Kaufman, Vice Chair
Omega Institute
150 Lake Drive
Rhinebeck, NY 12572
(845) 266-4444
e-mail: george@eomega.org

Another simple but potentially helpful book is Amiram Elwork's *Stress Management for Lawyers: How to Increase Personal and Professional Satisfaction in the Law*,[114] now in its second edition. Dr. Elwork is the Director of the Law-Psychology graduate program at Widener University in Wilmington, Delaware. The second edition added an insightful section on impaired lawyers by Douglas B. Marlowe, a lawyer-psychologist with the Treatment Research Institute of the University of Pennsylvania. Contact information:

Dr. Amiram Elwork
Widener University School of Law
P.O. Box 7475
Wilmington, DE 19803-7475
(302) 477-1213, ext. 1217

Dr. Douglas B. Marlowe
Treatment Research Institute
600 Public Ledge Building
150 South Independence Mall West
Philadelphia, PA 19106
(215) 399-0980

And finally, it should be encouraging that for every helping professional who has written a book or received national recognition there are dozens of others at the local or regional level who have also risen to the current challenge. Examples are Hindi Greenberg, described in a 1995 *Los Angeles Times* article as the "Ann Landers for lawyers;"[115] lawyer-therapist Richard A. Gottfried; and career consultant Martha Fay Africa, who have been helping lawyers in California for almost 20 years. Contact information:

Hindi Greenberg, President
Lawyers in Transition
P.O. Box 31026
San Francisco, CA 94131
(415) 285-5143
e-mail: hindi@lawyersintransition.com

Richard A. Gottfried
Licensed Marriage and Family Therapist
12304 Santa Monica Blvd., Suite 215
West Los Angeles, CA 90025
(310) 207-5177
e-mail:bi983@lafn.org

Martha Fay Africa
Major, Hagen & Africa
500 Washington Street, 5th Floor
San Francisco, CA 94111
(415) 956-1010
e-mail: mafrica@mhaglobal.com

Across the country in Boston, to mention two other examples, Sara Eddy, a former associate with a large firm, is now a practicing psychologist with the Law and Psychiatry Service at Massachusetts General Hospital; Leona Vogt has helped 2,000 unhappy lawyers through her career and management consulting business. Contact information:

Dr. Sara Eddy
Law and Psychiatry Service
Massachusetts General Hospital
60 Staniford Street, Suite 1
Boston, Massachusetts 02114
(617) 726-5924
e-mail: seddy@partners.org

Leona Vogt
Vogt Associates
50 Church Street
Cambridge MA 02138
(617)491-1191
e-mail: vogt@vogtassociates.com

The list of helping professionals reaching out specifically to lawyers could go on and on—and is growing to meet the increased need almost on a monthly basis. Nationally distributed publications on the subject, such as the ABA's 1997 book, *Living with the Law: Strategies to Avoid Burnout and Create Balance*, invariably bring new talent to our attention. In that particular publication, for example, we are introduced to Deborah K. Holmes, a Harvard Law graduate with Ernst & Young who has spent the past 15 years consulting with Fortune 500 and professional clients on how to balance professional and personal life; Preston K. Munter, M.D., a psychiatrist who serves as a consultant to the ABA on issues related to stress, depression, and professional burnout; Sheila Nielsen, cofounder of the "Part Time Lawyers Network" of the Chicago Bar Association and former executive director of the national association Lawyers for Alternative Work Schedules; and Margaret S. Spencer, who was a litigator with Shaw, Pittman, Potts and Trowbridge in Washington, D.C., for a number of years before turning her considerable talents to consulting. Ms. Spencer's other publications include *Time Management: An Essential Skill for the Successful Lawyer,* and *Time Management Habits: How to Develop Good Ones and Kick Bad Ones.*[116]

These encouraging professional stories and contributions are noted to ward off despair. We must not allow the troubling trends that clearly indicate less satisfaction and more dysfunction in the practicing bar to debilitate us. But neither must we allow these legitimate occasions for encouragement to serve as an excuse for complacency. We have no time for complacency. If we are to rescue and restore the legal profession—or the inherent satisfaction in what we have called LawyerLife—this is unequivocally a time for sustained action and principled reform. The right-minded lawyer will pay careful attention, whether motivated by altruistic concern for the profession or by pure self-interest, as we consider the finer points of the proposed rescue operation in subsequent chapters.

Notes

1. *Miserable With the Legal Life,* L.A. TIMES, June 27, 1995, at A1.
2. *See* DICK DAHL, *The Trouble With Lawyers,* BOSTON GLOBE MAGAZINE, Apr. 14, 1996, at 26.
3. *Id.*
4. MARY ANN GLENDON, A NATION UNDER LAWYERS 15 (1994).
5. SOL M. LINOWITZ (WITH MARTIN MAYER), THE BETRAYED PROFESSION: LAWYERING AT THE END OF THE TWENTIETH CENTURY 242 (1994).
6. BENJAMIN SELLS, THE SOUL OF THE LAW: UNDERSTANDING LAWYERS AND THE LAW 17 (1994).
7. *See* DEBORAH L. RHODE, IN THE INTERESTS OF JUSTICE: REFORMING THE LEGAL PROFESSION 8, 25, nn.18–20 (2000).
8. SELLS, *supra* note 6, at 34.
9. *Id.* at 17 (emphasis in original).
10. *See* WILLIAM W. EATON, J. C. ANTHONY, W. MANDEL & R. GARRISON, *Prevalence of Major Depression Disorder,* 32 J. OCCUPATIONAL MED. 1079 (1990).
11. *Id.* at 1081.
12. PATRICK J. SCHILTZ, *On Being a Happy, Healthy, and Ethical Member of an Unhappy, Unhealthy, and Unethical Profession,* 52 VAND. L. REV. , May 1999, at 871, 874.
13. *Id.*
14. WALT BACHMAN, LAW V. LIFE: WHAT LAWYERS ARE AFRAID TO SAY ABOUT THE LEGAL PROFESSION 22 (1995).
15. CONNIE J. A. BECK, BRUCE D. SALES & G. ANDREW H. BENJAMIN, *Lawyer Distress: Alcohol-Related Problems and Other Psychological Concerns Among a Sample of Practicing Lawyers,* 10 J. L. & HEALTH 1, 2 (1995–96).
16. RHODE, *supra* note 7, at 8.
17. *See* SCHILTZ, *supra* note 12, at 880; CARL HORN, *Twelve Steps Toward Fulfillment in Law Practice,* LAW PRAC. MGMT. , Oct. 1999, at 36–37. The North Carolina Chief Justice's Commission on Professionalism is in the process of updating the 1989 survey as this book goes to press. Interim results indicate that an even higher percentage of North Carolina lawyers are having suicidal ideation (about 20 percent), although three-quarters of these thought of suicide less than once a month (an option not recorded in the 1989 survey). Final results can be obtained by contacting Professor F. Leary Davis, Jr., at Campbell School of Law in Buies Creek, North Carolina.
18. RHODE, *supra* note 7, at 25.
19. AMERICAN BAR ASS'N, THE PULSE OF THE PROFESSION (Nov. 22, 2000).
20. *Id.* at 7.
21. *Id.* at 7–9, 16–20.
22. *Id.* at 7.

23. *Id.*
24. *Id.* at 28.
25. *Id.*
26. SELLS, *supra* note 6, at 34.
27. YOUNG LAWYERS DIV., AM. BAR ASS'N, THE STATE OF THE LEGAL PROFESSION 1990 (1991), at 1.
28. *Id.* at 13.
29. *Id.* at 81.
30. *Id.* at 52–53.
31. AMERICAN BAR ASS'N, AT THE BREAKING POINT: THE EMERGING CRISIS IN THE QUALITY OF LAWYERS' HEALTH AND LIVES AND ITS IMPACT ON LAW FIRMS AND CLIENT SERVICES (1991).
32. SCHILTZ, *supra* note 12, at 884 (footnotes omitted).
33. GLENDON, *supra* note 4, at 85.
34. MARYLAND STATE BAR ASS'N, REPORT OF THE COMMITTEE ON LAW PRACTICE QUALITY (1988).
35. HORN, *supra* note 17, at 36–37, reporting on the North Carolina Bar Association's *Report of the Quality of Life Task Force and Recommendations* (1991).
36. *Id.* at 37. As mentioned in note 17, the North Carolina Chief Justice's Commission on Professionalism is currently updating the 1989 findings. Interim results indicate about a 5-percent increase in the lawyers reporting that they were "very satisfied" *and* those reporting that they were "satisfied." However, there was also about a 4.6-percent increase in those describing themselves as "neutral" and approximately 13 percent still reporting that they were "dissatisfied" or "very dissatisfied."
37. *Id.*
38. *See* JULIE M. TAMMINEN, *Job Satisfaction Studies Signal a Need for Change, in* BREAKING TRADITIONS: WORK ALTERNATIVES FOR LAWYERS (Donna M. Killoughey ed., Am. Bar Ass'n, 1993), at 18–19.
39. GLENDON, *supra* note 4, at 85 (emphasis added).
40. *Miserable With the Legal Life, supra* note 1, at A16.
41. *Id.* at A1.
42. SCHILTZ, *supra* note 12.
43. *Id.* at. 882 (footnotes omitted).
44. *See* KATHLEEN E. HULL, *Cross-Examining the Myth of Lawyer Misery,* 52 VAND. L. REV., May 1999, at 971, 973.
45. SCHILTZ, *supra* note 12, at 884 n.92.
46. *See* SCHILTZ, *supra* note 12, at 885; HULL, *supra* note 44, at 974.
47. *See* text at notes 33–34.
48. MARYLAND STATE BAR ASS'N, 1998 MEMBERSHIP SURVEY (1998), at 6.
49. *See* HULL, *supra* note 44.
50. *Id.* at 971.

51. *Id.* at 972.
52. RHODE, *supra* note 7, at 8 (footnote omitted).
53. BACHMAN, *supra* note 14, at 12.
54. *Id.*
55. *See* text at notes 39–41. The quote is from a 1992 California Bar Association survey that found 70 percent of California lawyers would choose a different career if they could.
56. *See* text at note 37. The quotes, from HORN, *supra* note 17, at 36–37, are reporting findings of the North Carolina Bar Association's *Report of the Quality of Life Task Force and Recommendations* (1991).
57. *See* text at note 38.
58. *See* text at notes 33–34.
59. *See* text at note 9.
60. *See* text at note 52.
61. *See* text at note 38.
62. *See* DAHL, *supra* note 2, at 27.
63. *Id.* at 30.
64. *Id.*
65. *Miserable With the Legal Life, supra* note 1, at A16.
66. *See* DAHL, *supra* note 2, at 29.
67. *Id.*
68. *Id.*
69. RHODE, *supra* note 7, at 25. *Accord* BECK, *supra* note 15; R. LYNN PREGENZER, *Substance Abuse in the Legal Profession: A Symptom of Malaise,* 7 NOTRE DAME J.L. ETHICS & PUB. POL'Y 305–07 (1993); G. ANDREW, H. BENJAMIN *et al., The Prevalence of Depression, Alcohol Abuse and Cocaine Abuse Among United States Lawyers,* 13 INT'L J.L. & PSYCHIATRY 233, 240 (1990).
70. Beck, *supra* note 15, at 1.
71. *Id.* at 11.
72. SELLS, *supra* note 6, at 100, nn. 19–21 (citing surveys or studies in California, Oregon, Texas, and Georgia, and an ABA commission noting state bar estimates that "forty to seventy-five percent of all [disciplinary] complaints stem from lawyer impairment").
73. BECK, *supra* note 15, at 2.
74. *See* text at notes 9–15.
75. BACHMAN, *supra* note 14, at 22.
76. *See* text at notes 35–37.
77. HORN, *supra* note 17, at 37.
78. SELLS, *supra* note 6, at 99, citing G. ANDREW, H. BENJAMIN *et al., The Prevalence of Depression, Alcohol Abuse and Cocaine Abuse Among United States Lawyers,* 13 INT'L J.L. & PSYCHIATRY 233, 241 (1990); BECK, *supra* note 15, at 2.
79. BECK, *supra* note 15, at 2.

80. STEVEN KEEVA, TRANSFORMING PRACTICES: FINDING JOY AND SATISFACTION IN THE LEGAL LIFE (1999).
81. *Id.*
82. STEVEN KEEVA, *Passionate Practitioner,* A.B.A.J., June 2000, at 56.
83. *Id.*
84. *Id.* at 58.
85. *Id.*
86. *Id.* at 57.
87. *Id.* at 56.
88. *Id.*
89. *Id.*
90. KEEVA, *supra* note 80, at 37–40.
91. *Id.* at 40–41.
92. *Id.* at 42.
93. *Id.*
94. STEVEN KEEVA, *What Clients Want,* A.B.A.J., June 2001, at 48.
95. *Id.*
96. *Id.* at 51.
97. *Id.* at 52.
98. KEEVA, *supra* note 80, at 68–69.
99. *Id.* at 78–81.
100. *Id.* at 82.
101. *Id.*
102. *Id.*
103. STEVEN KEEVA, *The Nicest Tough Firm Around,* A.B.A.J., May 1999, at 61.
104. *Id.* at 62.
105. *Id.*
106. KEEVA, *supra* note 80, at 128.
107. STEVEN KEEVA, *Does Law Mean Never Having to Say You're Sorry?,* A.B.A.J. , Dec. 1999, at 64.
108. KEEVA, *supra* note 80, at 102-09.
109. *See* text in Chapter 1 at notes 59 through 65.
110. KEEVA, *supra* note 80, at 102.
111. *Id.* at 102–03.
112. *Id.* at 103.
113. GEORGE W. KAUFMAN, THE LAWYER'S GUIDE TO BALANCING LIFE AND WORK: TAKING THE STRESS OUT OF SUCCESS (1999).
114. AMIRAM ELWORK (WITH DOUGLAS R. MARLOWE), STRESS MANAGEMENT FOR LAWYERS: HOW TO INCREASE PERSONAL AND PROFESSIONAL SATISFACTION IN THE LAW, (2d ed.1997).
115. *Miserable With the Legal Life, supra* note 1, at A16.
116. *See* Living With the Law: Strategies to Avoid Burnout and Create Balance v–viii (Julie M. Tamminen ed., Am. Bar Ass'n 1997).

CHAPTER 3

Defining the Issues for a Profession "In Crisis"

In *Breaking Traditions: Work Alternatives for Lawyers*, Donna M. Killoughey concedes that "it has never been easy to practice law."[1] Nevertheless, she wrote in 1993, "20 or even 30 years ago it was at least predictable that a lawyer would:

- be fairly content practicing law;
- have a supportive network of family, professional colleagues, clients, and friends;
- be acquainted with adversaries and friends of adversaries;
- remain at the same place of employment for many years;
- make a good salary; and
- be respected in the community."[2]

In other words, as recently as the 1960s and 1970s, most lawyers were more or less satisfied with their professional lives. Few would have considered law to be a profession "in crisis."

As we have seen, it would be a mistake to regard this or any other earlier period as a "golden age." Real and sustainable improvements in the professional experience of the contemporary lawyer must look forward, not backward. However, the prudence that leads us to question uncritical nostalgia should not prevent our examining what was right or better about these earlier periods, either. And, as we should have also seen, there are many lessons we can glean from an historical perspective.

Take, for example, the inestimable value of a lawyer who also becomes a wise counselor—and even, as it often turned out, a trusted friend. Indeed, one wonders if it is not the increasing neglect of this single element of lawyering—and its replacement by what might be called the "Age of the Billable Hour"—that is most responsible for the "spiritual crisis" diagnosed by Yale Law School Dean Anthony Kronman.[3]

In defining the issues we face as a profession, this one looms large. But how in today's high-pressured climate—where there never seems to be enough time—can we realistically expect lawyers to offer not just technical assistance but also wise counsel? Or, for that matter, how can we expect a lawyer to tell a client who wants to "sue the bastards" and can pay the hourly rate that "they are damned fools and should stop"?[4] To answer these and related questions—about how to define or redefine the "common good," for example—we may need to engage in some hard, clear thinking about whether new boundaries to "zealous advocacy" should be fashioned and constructed.

In thinking through these admittedly complex issues, the power of moral suasion should not be underestimated. In other words, inspiring a lawyer to choose to do the right thing will often prove preferable to commanding it. After all, lawyers who considered theirs a high calling to public service and became "leaders in virtually all major movements for social reform in the nation's history"[5] are revered today because they freely chose the better part. They are not remembered as role models worthy of emulation because they were pressured or forced to give some portion of their professional or personal time to "*pro bono* work."

While the preference for voluntary choice does not apply in every instance, the closer a habit or practice gets to what we might consider "virtuous," the less likely we should make it the subject of de jure requirement. Take the laudable role of the lawyer as peacemaker,[6] or the lawyers Professor Bennett discovered "living lives dedicated to a higher purpose,"[7] or those Justice Holmes described as leading "a life of passion in the law,"[8] for example. None of these were the result of any law or rule or even any Code of Professional Responsibility. Rather, we honor their memory today because they freely chose, some at considerable sacrifice, the higher and better path.

The Profession-Versus-Business Debate

We have seen that concerns about "commercialization" of the legal profession were first expressed over a hundred years ago.[9] In 1895, a distinguished leader of the bar lamented that the "dignity and honor" of the profession was being contaminated by "the spirit of commerce."[10] For Henry Stimson, who served as secretary of war in both Roosevelt administrations and as secretary of state under Herbert Hoover, saving the bar from becoming "servants of business" took on almost patriotic overtones:

> I came to learn and understand the noble history of the profession of the law. I came to realize that without a bar trained in the conditions of courage and loyalty our constitutional theories of individual liberty would cease to be a living reality. . . . So I came to feel that the American lawyer should regard himself as a potential officer of his government and a defender of its laws and Constitution. I felt that if the time should ever come when this tradition had faded out and the members of the bar had become *merely the servants of business*, the future of our liberties would be gloomy indeed.[11]

Less patriotic but equally forceful was Supreme Court Justice Harlan Fisk Stone's previously noted complaint, made in the 1930s, that lawyers had become "obsequious servants of business . . . tainted by the morals and manners of the marketplace. . . . "[12]

Fast-forward to the recent past and complaints about the commercialization of law are still being registered—and, in a sense, with greater justification. In *Law v. Life: What Lawyers Are Afraid to Say About the Legal Profession*, for example, Walt Bachman rightly complains that "[a] stunningly capable lawyer is less favored" in the contemporary practice "than a more mediocre marketing whiz."[13] For Bachman, who has since left the practice to write and teach, the distinction lies at the heart of why he chose to become a lawyer. "When I opted for law school over an MBA," he writes, "I thought I was leaving the economically driven hurly-burly of the business world for a dignified profession, a distinction becoming more and more blurred each year."[14]

As noted in chapter 2, the ABA's "Pulse Study," which involved lawyers at all stages of practice in cities in three different parts of the country, identified "Financial Pressures Turning Law Into a Business, Not a Profession" as "Pressure Point #1."[15] The November 2000 report detailed the specific concerns of those who participated in the 14 focus groups conducted earlier that year. Among them:

- Managing partners take on more work so that profit levels can be maintained.
- Everyone is expected to produce more.

- The general professional atmosphere is more businesslike and less congenial.
- Less time is spent on nonbillable efforts, including mentoring and "work for the greater good."
- Young lawyers may be required to meet ambitious billable-hour goals to justify their salaries.
- Lawyers also are expected to be "rainmakers" earlier on in their careers.
- The focus becomes business development and quickly churning work, not larger aims.
- Firm decision-makers must focus on running the business, not practicing law.
- Significant pressure is placed on young lawyers, who are expected to begin soliciting business *and* learn the nuts and bolts of how to practice law on their own shortly after they join a firm.[16]

Or, as one of the participants more poignantly summed it up, "I think the practice of law has become the business of law, and it's a grind."[17]

On the other hand, before we have too unmitigated a pity party, a few qualifying points are in order. First, to some extent there has always been a business element to the practice of law. Office space must be obtained, upfitted, furnished, expanded, and so on. Personnel must be hired, managed, and paid; employment and other taxes withheld; benefits fairly apportioned under complex federal regulations; and so forth. Office equipment and technology is ever changing and always more expensive. And all this requires a great deal of money, however professional, wise, or dignified the lawyers are who must ultimately generate it.

Second, as Harvard Law Professor Mary Ann Glendon reminds us, the very "idea that law is not a business, or only 'incidentally' so, was a conceit seized upon by elite attorneys in the early years of the [Twentieth century] to distance themselves from their buccaneer predecessors and from 'hustling' immigrant lawyers, as well as to assert their independence from their own clients."[18] Professor Glendon faults the "careless use of 'commercial' as an epithet [as] mischievous," that is, as resting "either on the arrogant assumption that businesspeople have no ethics or on the dubious proposition that businesspeople invariably place short-term profits ahead of all other considerations."[19] Glendon agrees "that lawyers assume higher responsibilities toward those they represent than businesspersons do toward customers," but correctly objects to the "cramped concepts of business ethics" that are often assumed in complaints about "commercialization."[20]

Third, the current environment, in which many firms pay top dollar to associates and then work them to death to "turn a profit," is a vicious cycle that grew out of—or dramatically escalated during—the "freakish law boom of the 1980s."[21] In other words, the seeds of certain of the maladies about which many now complain were sewn in a period when lawyers and law firms were making unprecedented amounts of money, a period many assumed was here to stay. But then, alas, as Professor Glendon describes it, "the binge of the 1980s gave way to the hangover of the 1990s."[22]

Whatever qualifications may be appropriate, however, there are many lawyers today who remain trapped in this metaphorical "hangover." In some ways the remedy is quite simple. As the nursery aphorism goes, "All work and no play makes Jack a dull boy." And today there are far too many dull lawyers, exhausted yet never feeling really caught up, who desperately need to learn how to "play" again.

Reflecting on the real-life effects of billable hours requirements on the associates at many large firms, Ambassador Sol M. Linowitz captures the opportunity costs of contemporary "success":

> At the large firms, associates are now expected to "fill the book" (show time sheets involving two thousand hours a year of work for clients). If the lawyer takes the normal ten holidays and a minimal two weeks' vacation, this demand works out to forty-two *billable* hours a week, which implies fifty or even sixty hours a week *at the office*. The associates in the large firms cannot play the piano or paint a picture or act in a church play because they simply don't have the time.[23]

In Linowitz' analysis, excessive hours not only inhibit personal balance and growth, but also have negative consequences on *professional* development:

> The tragedy is that, in the end, the single-minded drive toward winning the competitions at the firm will make these young lawyers not only less useful citizens, less interesting human beings, and less successful parents but also less good as lawyers, less sympathetic to other people's troubles, and less valuable to their clients.[24]

If Ambassador Linowitz is correct on the latter point—that more balance yields better lawyers—perhaps a measure of encouragement can be drawn from the convergence of personal and long-term professional interests.

At the same time, the pressures driving the contemporary practice, particularly in medium-size and large law firms, are undeniably complex and will therefore defy simplistic solutions. Individual lawyers may choose to work less and make less money, or even leave the practice altogether in search of a kinder and gentler life, but the law firm's options are more limited. This is true, as Stanford Law Professor Deborah L. Rhode has observed, because complaints about "decline in professionalism," including complaints about commercialization, "partly reflect structural changes in the market for legal services."[25] These changes, many of which can be traced directly back to the boom market of the 1980s, include increases in the number of lawyers competing for available business, increased "[p]rice consciousness among corporate clients," substantial decreases in loyalty between lawyers and clients and lawyers and their own partners, and the trend toward an "eat-what-you-kill" approach to firm compensation.[26]

We began this chapter with Donna Killoughey's observation that as recently as the 1960s and 1970s most lawyers would expect, *inter alia*, to "remain at the same place of employment for many years."[27] In sharp contrast is Professor Rhode's account of frayed relations and frequent partings in the contemporary practice:

> Legal practice has become more competitive within as well as among law firms. A steady rise in costs, coupled with instability in demand, have led to greater insecurity in private practice. More public information about law firm salaries has intensified financial rivalries and lateral defections. . . . Partnership means less and is harder to obtain. As the likelihood of promotion diminishes, the competition among lawyers intensifies. Incoming associates are wined and dined, then worked to death. At senior levels, less productive partners may be squeezed out. Productive ones may be lured away.[28]

Whether this relatively new competitiveness and insecurity inside many firms is inevitable social Darwinism or avoidable through a conscious shift in priorities is debatable, but one conclusion is certain: The security of "a supportive network of professional colleagues,"[29] another of the predictable expectations of practice in the 1960s and 1970s identified by Ms. Killoughey, has become increasingly elusive.

Lawyer-turned-psychotherapist Benjamin Sells regularly sees the profound effects of these fundamental changes on his lawyer patients. Understanding the professionwide trend as "ignor[ing] more personal aspects of partnership and focus[ing] instead on defining partnership in terms of property interests," with "many law firms believ[ing] they exist for one purpose only—to make the maximum amount of money," Dr. Sells issues a plaintive cry for a return to a more nurturing balance:

> What I hear repeatedly from today's lawyers is a longing for partnership to mean that they really are part of something communal, something that identifies them as standing shoulder to shoulder with others in a joint endeavor, something that means as partners they will fall heir to the traditions of their particular firm and that they will help to create a legacy for heirs yet to come.[30]

Of course, this is not what many find in firms where the bottom line overshadows almost everything else. Rather, as Sells notes in *The Soul of the Law: Understanding Lawyers and the Law*, "[I]t is becoming distressingly commonplace to value people solely on their current money-making potential with little if any attention being given to nonmonetary factors—length of service, ability to teach and mentor new lawyers, involvement in bar and civic activities, and the like."[31]

This money-is-all-that-really-matters approach is "saddest and most disgraceful" when applied to "a lawyer [who] gets on in years and begins to slow down a bit."[32] Sells reports:

> I have heard numerous stories of lawyers with thirty or more years of experience being shuttled into smaller offices, having their secretaries either taken away or assigned additional duties, and effectively (if oh, so subtly) being snubbed within the firm. The bottom line says you matter only as long as you produce, that you are what you earn; to paraphrase Descartes, "I produce therefore I am."[33]

The psychological and emotional effects of this kind of treatment, particularly when it follows years of productivity and "success," are not at all surprising. Again Dr. Sells reports what he hears and observes in his clinical practice:

> Increasingly, people are running into a kind of psychic wall. Often this happens in midlife or later, but it can happen any time. After thirty

> years with a firm, a partner is asked to leave because his billings are down. After taking time off from her career to raise a family and make a home, a mother encounters the incredible fact of a legal profession actually *antagonistic* to her reentry into the workplace. Or a forty-year-old in perfect health suddenly becomes depressed and unable to concentrate on his work. When such walls are hit, questions long dormant revive. What does it all mean? Is this all there is? Have I been doing the wrong thing all these years?[34]

These kinds of experiences often result in the dissatisfaction and dysfunction discussed in the last chapter. They also lead an increasing number, in the words of U.S. Circuit Judge Laurence H. Silberman, to "hate what the practice of law has become."[35]

Keeping in mind that our modest goal at this point is simply to *define the issues*, one might reasonably hope for broad agreement on at least what *questions* we should be asking. Although there is an unavoidable business element in the practice of law, what steps can be taken to recapture the sincere personal warmth that attended professional relationships a few short decades ago? Even if we concede market-driven "structural changes,"[36] can we resurrect to any significant degree the "supportive network of professional colleagues"[37] our recent forbears (and some of us) have enjoyed? While most would reject the crass notion that "law firms exist for one purpose only—to make the maximum amount of money,"[38] how *should* human qualities (like loyalty and compassion, for example) be factored into what often appear to be intractable "economic realities"?

These are not simple questions and they certainly defy simplistic answers or solutions, but there should be no doubt that we must give high priority to addressing them. And, if our efforts are to be successful, nothing is more important than regaining the kind of work/personal life balance enjoyed by our professional predecessors even a few decades ago.

In Search of Balance

At the 1996 meeting of the Women's Bar Association of Massachusetts, where the theme was "The Misery Factor," it was not "failures in court [o]r the pain and suffering of clients . . . [o]r even the dismal public reputation [of lawyers]"[39] on which attention focused. Rather, the increasing "misery" was attributed to the mind-numbing number of hours many lawyers are choosing, or being forced, to spend on their work.[40]

Martin L. Aronson, a partner in a successful Boston firm, related to those present how billing pressures eroded his daughter's initial enthusiasm for the practice of law. Having won the intense competition and "landed a job at a prestigious Washington, D.C., law firm fresh out of law school," it did not take this bright, young lawyer long to realize that her expectation of intellectual stimulation and professional independence were irreconcilable with the reality of her life as human capital in a multimillion-dollar business operation.

"She started to become swallowed up—that is the image I have: literally swallowed up—by what I saw as the large-firm machinery, by the billable hours." As reported in *The Boston Globe Magazine*, Aronson continued:

> She was becoming obsessed with the necessity of cranking out a certain amount of billable hours a week, a month, a year. Her supervising partners didn't seem concerned about the quality of her work, just the "billables." I watched a personality transformation. . . . I could hear her voice on the phone growing thinner and thinner, until she quit the firm and took a job with a government agency.[41]

Unfortunately, the speaker drew a picture and described a progression, or perhaps a regression, which is becoming all too familiar.

It is this double whammy—excessive "billable-hours" requirements and the spoken or unspoken priority given *quantity* over *quality* of work—that is making many lawyers unhappy. Some, like David A. Deakin, who found his work as a law clerk at a large firm "sort of soul-destroying" and elected to take a public service job making less than half as much money after graduating from Harvard Law School, quality of life choices are made at the outset of a career. Many others, for a variety of reasons, can or do not make these choices initially, but find themselves experiencing "the epidemiology of what the Japanese call *karoshi*, death from overwork,"[43] some months or years later.

Michael Traynor, then a partner in a San Francisco firm, has noted what should be obvious: that "karoshi" is inconsistent with having a meaningful life, outside of work—or even, for that matter, with basic good health. Responding to Professor Patrick J. Schiltz's lead article in the May 1999 issue of the *Vanderbilt Law Review* ("On Being a Happy, Healthy, and Ethical Member of an Unhappy, Unhealthy, and

Unethical Profession"), Traynor comments on the lack of balance, health, and personal happiness that may lie down the road for many "successful" lawyers.

> The pressure to bill hours and collect bills is unrelenting and increasing. There will be times when you are in the office at night or on a Sunday afternoon, alone or among a few others, marveling at the hours your fellow lawyers in firms across the country are racking up in trials or transactions or on their home computers. It is difficult to attain 1700 to 1800 actual billable hours a year, let alone 2000, or 2400, or more, and have reasonable time for family, relationships, and other pursuits.
>
> For perspective, consider a 25-year-old lawyer who bills 2400 hours a year for 20 years, a total of 48,000 hours at an average billable rate over that span of $300 per hour. At age 45, that lawyer may inventory his life: gross billings, $14.4 million; at or near the top of the pyramid structure that supports what Professor Schiltz describes as the "skim"; divorced; estranged from children; hypertense; depressed; a reputation as a hardball player; transitory transactional relationships; a luxurious home and car plus a sport utility vehicle; an ample taste for fine wines and cigars; and a question: What have I done with my life?[44]

Indeed, as Professor Rhode poignantly puts it, "for too many practitioners, 'quality of life' is a nonissue. 'What life?'"[45] Writing in 2000, Rhode elaborated:

> Billable hour requirements have increased dramatically over the last two decades, and what has not changed is the number of hours in the day. Almost half of private practitioners now bill at least nineteen hundred hours per year, and to do so honestly they frequently need to work sixty-hour weeks. Especially in large firms, where hourly demands can be even higher, all work and no play is fast becoming the norm rather than the exception.[46]

It is almost tragic that many who read Michael Traynor's comment (noting that it is "difficult to attain 1700 to 1800 actual billable hours a year") or Professor Rhode's (noting that "[a]lmost half of private practitioners now bill at least 1,900 hours per year") will find themselves longing for the "good old days" when *only* 1700 to 1900 hours were expected.

The precise number of billable hours that are expected or actually worked is less important than the fundamental fact that the increasingly long hours are simply unhealthy. Nevertheless, there have been a number of studies in the past 15 years or so that confirm escalating billable hours expectations and output, and the figures are alarming.

As Professor Schiltz reports, as recently as the late 1960s "most partners billed between 1200 and 1400 hours per year and most associates between 1400 and 1600 hours."[47] But, oh, what a difference a few decades make!

If the reader will pardon a personal note, 1200 to 1600 annual billable hours was roughly where the "larger" firms in Charlotte, North Carolina, were when your author entered practice in 1976. Although time sheets were submitted each day in our firm of 13 partners and four associates—then one of the three largest firms in Charlotte, which now has at least ten law firms with over 100 lawyers, several with over 200, and satellite offices of a number of national firms—there were no billable hours *requirements*. Senior partners in our firm, four out of five of whom graduated from Harvard or Yale Law School, made good livings, but they also chaired nonprofit boards, led the Charlotte Symphony and Opera, were active and interested in local politics, were leaders of the state and local bar, and had plenty of time for friends and family. Even as a young associate, I was able to lead a church youth group, exercise regularly, do some satisfying *pro bono* work for our county historical preservation society, spend ample time with our growing family, and generally "have a life" outside the office.

Not so for almost half the associates in private practice in 1991 who "billed at least 2000 hours during both 1989 and 1990" or the "fifth [who] billed at least 2400 hours in 1990."[48] A study conducted by William Ross in 1993 found "that 51 percent of associates and 23 percent of partners billed at least 2000 hours in 1993."[49] A survey by Altman Weil Pensa "found that the median number of billable hours for associates in firms of all sizes in 1995 was 1823; 25 percent of associates billed 1999 hours or more, and 19 percent billed at least 2166 hours."[50] Writing in *The Soul of the Law*, Benjamin Sells notes summarily that "[b]illable hour requirements for lawyers in law firms have almost doubled in the last 15 years, now averaging 2000 to 2500 hours per year."[52]

It is crucial to keep in mind as billable hours are discussed, assuming you are an honest lawyer, that there is "a big difference—a painfully big difference between the hours that you will *bill* and the hours you will *spend at work.*"[53] Professor Schiltz, who was a Supreme Court law clerk and then practiced law in a large Midwestern firm before joining the Notre Dame law faculty, hits this point dead center:

> Obviously, you will not be able to bill the time that you spend on vacation, or in bed with the flu, or at home waiting for the plumber. But you will also not be able to bill for much of what you will do at the office or during the workday—going to lunch, chatting with your co-workers about the latest office romance, visiting your favorite web sites, going down the hall to get a cup of coffee, reading your mail, going to the bathroom, attending the weekly meeting of your practice group, filling out your time sheet, talking with your spouse on the phone, sending e-mail to friends, preparing a "pitch" for a prospective client, getting your hair cut, attending a funeral, photocopying your tax returns, interviewing a recruit, playing Solitaire on your computer, doing *pro bono* work, reading advance sheets, taking a summer associate to a baseball game, attending CLE seminars, writing a letter about a mistake in your credit card bill, going to the dentist, dropping off your dry cleaning, daydreaming, and so on.[54]. . .

Professor Carl T. Bogus, who practiced for 18 years before entering academia, makes the same basic point in "The Death of an Honorable Profession," and then clearly describes the severe personal consequences of annual billable time requirements in excess of 1800 hours.

> To extrapolate how many hours lawyers work per day from the total billable hours per year, assume that, on average, lawyers: (1) convert 70 percent of their work time into billable hours; (2) do not work on eight public holidays; and (3) take a total of three weeks per year for vacations, personal, and sick days. Based on these assumptions, lawyers generating 1500 billable hours per year—the average when computerized timekeeping was introduced—need to work either nine hours per day, five days a week, or seven and half hours per day, six days a week. Those are long hours, for lawyers or members of any other occupation. . . .
>
> Once we move beyond perhaps 1800 billable hours per year, however, we are entering different terrain. A lawyer working six days a week needs to work ten hours a day to produce 2000 billable hours per year, 11 hours a day to produce 2200, and 12 hours a day to produce 2400. While people may work oppressively long hours in short bursts, it is impossible to work these kinds of hours—day in and day out, year in and year out—and maintain a personal life. For example, a lawyer billing 2200 hours a year

> who left home at 8:00 A.M. every morning and had a half-hour commute to work would not arrive home until 8:00 P.M., six days a week.[55]

Message to the profession: whatever the subtleties or complexities of law firm economics in the twenty-first century, sweatshop hours like these are unhealthy and intolerable. Indeed, even if an individual lawyer is willing to work these oppressively long hours, appropriate concern for his or her mental and emotional health requires intervention to *prevent* it.

In short, as Judge Silberman put it, hours which a decade or two ago "would have [been] thought unbearable"[56] have now become almost commonplace. Of course, that excessive hours are increasingly the norm does not make them any less oppressive. To the contrary, we have seen that the "increasingly long workdays with decreasing time for personal and family life"[57] is at the very heart of current lawyer discontent, leading to complaints about "living to work rather than working to live"[58]—or, as a 1991 ABA report put it, about being "asked not [only] to *dedicate*, but to *sacrifice* their lives to the firm."[59]

Once again, there is likely to be some disagreement about how many billable hours are too many, how escalating associate salaries factor into moral imperatives governing humane working conditions, and about the collateral consequences of specific remedies or proposals. Happily, however, at this point the goal is simply to define the issues, and it remains reasonable to hope for broad agreement at least about what *questions* we should be asking.

For example, at a time when a majority agree that their legal careers are "putting too much of a burden on their personal lives,"[60] what can law firms and the organized bar do to help restore a healthier balance? How many billable hours are reasonable at different phases and stages of a lawyer's career and personal life? Chief Justice William H. Rehnquist, writing in 1987, complained that a law firm requiring its associates to bill more than 2000 hours a year "is treating the associate very much as a manufacturer would treat a purchase of one hundred tons of scrap metal."[61] If law firms have no more regard for their professional employees than to regard them as expendable human capital, as the chief justice appears to be suggesting, should they be subject to increased regulatory scrutiny—just like any other business whose practices are potentially dangerous to its employees or customers? How, in the single-minded push to maximize firm revenue by increasing the *quantity* of hours billed, do we as a profession continue to give proper attention to the *quality* of our work? And what can be done to restore the mentoring by experienced lawyers of their younger colleagues, a rich and venerable tradition that these days is often praised but much less regularly practiced?

In addressing these and related issues—collectively referred to in the 1991 ABA report as "the time famine"[62]—we would do well to "think outside the box." The current pattern of escalating salaries followed by excessive work demands followed by increasing dissatisfaction and even burnout is a huge problem with complex origins (including, of course, basic human greed). Thinking outside the box, how might the creative work and compensation arrangements discussed in the last part of this chapter, and in more detail in chapters 5 and 6, serve as partial solutions to what appear at times to be intractable problems? If we ultimately embrace part-time, flex-time, or other more-flexible work arrangements, how do we ensure quality work *and* fair compensation? And above all, how do we "pursue excellence" not only in what we do professionally, but also in the larger context of who we are as family, as friends, and as citizens?

Does Size of Firm Matter?

A growing body of anecdotal and research data suggests that LawyerLife is in most distress, although by strictly financial measures it is most successful, in the large-firm practice. Although large firms continue to attract a significant percentage of the most-accomplished law school graduates and are not without their defenders, they have received consistent criticism since the early 1990s.

Traditionally, the largest firms have disproportionately chosen their associates among top graduates of the most elite law schools. Therefore, it should have set off major alarms when Yale Law School Dean Anthony Kronman advised young lawyers to "stay clear of . . . large firm practice [as pejoratively described in a previous chapter of his book]."[63] Writing in 1993, Dean Kronman suggests as alternatives:

- the smaller firms that have been created by the unhappy refugees from the larger ones, eager to establish an environment in which the intrinsic pleasures of law practice are more highly valued;[64] or
- the general-practice law firm in a small town or city outside the country's largest metropolitan centers.[65]

Although Dean Kronman is ultimately pessimistic that "the mass of students at our best law schools" will be able to resist the allure of "the money and prestige of large-firm practice,"[66] he nevertheless delivers his counsel forcefully and unequivocally.

Dean Kronman's advice is consistent with a growing number of anecdotes and "war stories" from the large-firm front lines. Cynthia J. Cohen, who left a large Boston firm in 1985 to establish a litigation practice with two other large-firm "refugees," attended the 20th reunion of her Harvard Law School class (in 1995), and came away with the "impression that quite a few of [her] classmates in large law firms were quite unhappy."[67] Sara Eddy, a former associate with another large Boston firm who is now a psychologist with Massachusetts General Hospital's "Law and Psychiatry Services," reports what she sees in her clinical practice:

> The typical path of a lawyer's career gives good cause to feel unhappy, Eddy says, because of a series of brutal "winnowings" that begin in law school. First, law students seek the grades that will get them on the law review, with the advantages this will give them in future job searches. Then they compete to land prestigious summer-associate jobs after their second year. Then, it's the bar exam and competition for the first full-time job. And then, Eddy says, it starts all over again with the pressure to make partner. "You're constantly looking over your shoulder to see who's behind you; you're constantly looking ahead to see where you're going. It's a very difficult process to be in. It's hard to relax."[68]

Although merely anecdotal, the accounts of Cohen, Eddy, and others corroborate research showing that associates and partners in large firms are less satisfied with their professional lives than are lawyers in smaller firms or other work arrangements.

Since 1995, when Walt Bachman published *Law v. Life: What Lawyers Are Afraid to Say About the Legal Profession,*[69] lawyers who have tried large-firm practice and found it wanting have been increasingly willing to tell their stories publicly. And thankfully, their tales are often told with sufficient style and laced with ample humor to make what could be intolerably bitter pills easier to swallow.

Bachman, who chose to return to his Midwestern roots after receiving law degrees from Oxford University (where he was a Rhodes Scholar) and Stanford, initially accepted a position as an associate with a prominent Minneapolis firm. But unlike some unhappy associates in large firms, who linger on for years in the "slough of despond,"[70] Bachman's response to life as a large-firm associate was swift and sure. As he tells his story:

> On my third successive weekend researching the esoteric points of the Internal Revenue Code's application to a multinational corporation, staring at the law firm library wall, I impulsively decided that hanging out my shingle for divorce clients on Lake Street, a somewhat tawdry Minneapolis thoroughfare bordered by used car lots and massage parlors, would be better than this. I quit on the spot, without the slightest idea what I would be able to line up for myself.[71]

As it turned out, the young Bachman went on to have a distinguished, if varied, legal career as a prosecutor, state bar executive, and senior partner in his own law firm, before leaving practice altogether for the gentler pursuits of writing, teaching, and public service.

Jonathan Foreman and Cameron Stracher are two others who have written eloquently and with a healthy dose of humor about their experiences as large-firm associates. Foreman, writing in the Winter 1997 issue of New York's *City Journal* describes his Wall Street firm as a "machine" with "irrational hierarchies, institutionalized bullying, and overwhelming peer pressure."[72] Hopefully waxing into hyperbole, Foreman reports that "[c]apricious tyrants roamed the hallways," that "[t]hose who flourished in the system were almost always monsters, twisted into Balzacian shapes by the struggle for power," and that the firm was generally "a petri dish for the growth of abnormal psychologies."[73]

Foreman concluded that associates in his firm were "wage slaves, members of a white-collar proletariat" over whom management maintained almost absolute control. He was "called at 3:00 A.M. on Saturday and ordered to go to the office for some proofreading."[74] One of his fellow associates "was forced to miss his sister's wedding."[75] And for all of them, "[d]ay/night, weekend/weekday were distinctions that had lost all meaning."[76]

To say that the picture Foreman draws is not pretty is an understatement. But perhaps most galling is the deceptive way promising law students were reportedly wined, dined, and entertained, but once they accepted the firm's offer of employment, soon woke up to the harsh reality of an endless stream of "mindless, repetitious, stunningly dull work."[77] To survive emotionally, the associates secretly caballed, routinely referring to their oppressors by nicknames like "Dave the

Barracuda" and "Caligula" (the Roman emperor known for torture and extraordinary cruelty).[78] Not surprisingly, over a period of several years, Foreman and many of his compatriots chose to leave for more-humane employment.

Cameron Stracher, who has written a book[79] and a piece for *The Wall Street Journal*[80] on his experience as a large-firm associate, tells a remarkably similar story. Having "graduated Harvard Law School at the beginning of a decade of diminished expectations" (the 1990s), Stracher was one of about 50 associates to accept an offer of employment that particular year from a large New York firm with twice as many associates as partners.[81] In sharp contrast to *the expectation* of partnership into the 1970s, because only one to three made partner each year, associates realized from the outset that their "chance of becoming a partner was approximately five percent."[82]

Stracher soon came to understand the pyramid structure of the large firm as "a giant Ponzi scheme" with partner profits depending upon "an unending source of the associates entering at the bottom of the pyramid, funneling cash up the chain, and departing before making partner."[83] Nevertheless, like Jonathan Foreman, having worked so hard to get there, Stracher remained with the firm almost three years—years made up of "11-hour days and at least one weekend day," often working "past midnight and through the weekend. Dinner was eaten from a plastic tin in a conference room. Home was an office down the hall."[84] And that was billing only the minimum 2,000 hours; "[m]any associates bill[ed] 2,500 hours, 3,000 hours, and more."[85]

As bad as the hours were, the thoughtless way "the grunts at the bottom"[86] were treated, and the dull and often useless assignments they were given, were even worse. As Stracher initially considered whether to leave the firm (after about two years), his thoughts were far from the intellectually stimulating work and professionally satisfying environment he had expected. Instead, his memories were of clerical work cataloging documents "which should have been done years earlier, yet . . . was unnecessary;" of working all weekend on an assignment a partner had thoughtlessly forgotten to tell him was no longer necessary; and of "countless hours" spent doing research that was billed to clients with deep pockets, but "rarely, if ever, used."[87] On the relational side, he remembered no "close friendships . . . forged; [no] attempt among the lawyers to connect,"[88] nor even any expression of gratitude for his "rigorous work."[89] Not surprisingly, before the end of the third year, Stracher and roughly half of his "class" left the firm. Most of the rest would either follow or become permanent associates over the next two years.

Although the firms for which Foreman and Stracher worked were apparently extreme even for large firms, a growing body of research indicates that associates *and partners* in large firms are unhappier than their counterparts in smaller firms or other work arrangements. On one level, this is not a difficult concept: When all you do during most waking hours is work, work, work, exhaustion and a sense of having "no life" are inevitable. In fact, we should worry about any lawyer honestly billing more than 1800 hours a year who is *not* concerned about the opportunity costs inherent in tending to the "jealous mistress."

With "the general rule of thumb [being] the bigger the firm, the longer the hours."[90] Professor Schiltz elaborates:

> For example, a recent study found that over 41 percent of associates in firms of under 101 lawyers billed fewer than 1800 hours, as compared to about 16 percent of associates in firms of over 250 lawyers. At the same time, almost 27 percent of associates in the smaller firms billed over 1900 hours, as compared to approximately 36 percent of associates in the larger firms. At the biggest firms in the biggest cities, associates commonly bill 2000 to 2500 hours per year. Big firm partners do not have it much better. Junior partners at the nation's 125 largest law firms average 1955.5 billable hours per year, almost 300 hours per year more than partners in small firms. At some big firms, the average number of hours billed by partners and associates alike is 2000.[91]

Not surprisingly, clocking hours like these results in correspondingly high percentages of large-firm associates and partners complaining about having too little time for family, friends, or themselves. Again, Professor Schiltz reports:

> While roughly half of all attorneys in private practice complain about not having enough time for themselves and their families, in big firms the proportion of similarly disaffected lawyers is about three-quarters. The ABA's survey of young lawyers in 1995 found that 62 percent of those working in firms of at least 150 lawyers were dissatisfied with the amount of time they had to work, while only 28 percent of those working in firms of fewer than seven lawyers had the same complaint.[92]

Or, as Professor Rhode succinctly puts it, "profit-driven pyramids come at a price."[93] And, unfortunately, the price in many cases includes the large-firm lawyer's quality of life outside of work.

Although it had a low response rate (11 percent), a 1997 *National Law Journal* poll of partners in the nation's 125 largest firms confirmed the discontent of those who did respond. As reported in a front-page article titled "Big-Firm Partners: Profession Sinking,"[94] 82.7 percent "believe the profession has changed for the worse. Private practice has turned sour, partners say, because the law has become a fiercely dollar-driven business."[95] For 73 percent of the respondents—and 83 percent of female partners—"their workloads prevent[ed] them from spending enough time with family and friends."[96] Almost 43 percent "reported that their job had hurt their relationship with a significant other" and 66.6 percent "said they had no time to pursue hobbies or other interests."[97] And this is the pinnacle of "success," the place at which the best and brightest in our profession hope to one day arrive?

On the other hand, we must avoid processing all this negative information about LawyerLife in the large firm in too simplistic a manner. As we have seen, the increased demands and pressure of large firm practice did not occur in a vacuum, but to a significant degree have been market driven. Since the New York firms increased starting salaries for top law school graduates to a whopping $15,000 in the 1970s, compensation for first-year associates has climbed astonishingly. And while it is hard to feel too sorry for the large-firm partners at the top of the pyramid who long wistfully for the good-old-days when they could take home a million a year, it is also a bit much to hear an associate making $125,000 to $175,000 per year whine about having to work too much. And yet. . . .

Those who believe the large firm option is potentially a beneficial way to practice law have to be concerned about the anecdotal and survey-based indicia of discontent and record-low morale. And, in fact, the organized bar does appear to be increasingly aware of the problem, and there have been scattered efforts to address it. For example, when a 1997 survey of Boston lawyers found associates in large firms the least happy of the eight categories studied, the Boston Bar Association's "Task Force on Professional Fulfillment" promptly issued its report, "Expectations, Reality, and Recommendations for Change." *The Wall Street Journal* reported in 1999 on what some large firms are doing to counter the "exodus of young lawyers who are turned off by the grind of big-time practice."[98] And the ABA's 2000 Pulse Study minced no words in reporting that "[t]he least satisfied lawyers [encountered in the 14 "focus groups"] were young lawyers who worked for large Chicago firms,"[99] or ironically, that "[t]he only group who appeared *unconvinced* of the need for balance were firm decision-makers representing medium- to large-sized law firms in Chicago."[100]

The ABA's Pulse Study summed up the vicious cycle—the debt-driven need for a high salary leading to unreasonable work demands leading to discontent or worse—in which many associates in large law firms have found themselves:

> Young attorneys are often attracted to these positions because the high salaries allow them to more quickly pay off debts owed for law school. . . . Yet these same attorneys, many of whom were the best and the brightest in their respective law school classes, find practicing law in a large law firm anything but stimulating. Their high salaries necessitate that firms set 1900+ billable hour goals that they must meet to stay employed. To meet these requirements, they are often holed up in their office reviewing documents on their computer for significant stretches of time, with little contact with clients or little opportunity to learn about more stimulating facets of practicing law. . . . What's sobering to consider is that, in many ways, these attorneys represent some of the brightest young minds in the profession. And yet their initial foray into law may be so negative that many will abandon the profession as soon as law school debts are paid off.[101]

As one associate in an ABA focus group put it, "This is going to sound so cynical, but my career goal is to pay off my debt."[102] Amazingly, this young lawyer—a "New Bar Admittee [who graduated from law school with] over $100,000 in debt"—was already so unhappy that he was considering going "back to manual labor like [he] did before [he] went to law school . . . once [he gets his] debt paid off."[103]

While some large law firms and portions of the organized bar are beginning to wake up to the apparent misery of a significant number of young lawyers, others remain detached or unconvinced. Some correctly observe that the almost absurdly high starting salaries do not "grow on trees," that is, that revenues must be generated to support them. This is undeniably true, but in the face of widespread unhappiness, do economic realities justify the callousness of one "Firm Decision-maker" quoted in the ABA Pulse Study? When asked what was being done "to help young attorneys in his firm have a balanced life," this firm's "Caligula" responded:

> We try to push them to work harder, actually. We're not trying to make their lives easier. By nature, I don't think everyone is necessarily com-

> mitted. I think that's something that develops over time with maturity, commitment to the job, whatever the job is. At the same time, you want to try to keep their feet on the ground. Generally, I think you need to kick them in the ass to get them interested in the first place.[104]

If attitudes like this "Firm Decision-maker's" become widespread, perhaps one day we will not only be reporting lawyer suicides, but also lawyer murders!

As individual firms and the bar collectively consider how to encourage better balance—and we absolutely must as a profession *insist* upon it—we should keep in mind that large-firm practice is a relatively recent phenomenon. As late as 1948, more than 60 percent of all lawyers were solo practitioners.[105] In the early 1960s, "there were only 38 firms in the entire country with more than 50 lawyers,"[106] and even as recently as 1975, "there were fewer than four dozen firms with more than 100 lawyers, totaling 6,558 lawyers in all."[107] Three years later, in 1978, there were 15 firms in the country "with 200 or more lawyers, and approximately 3,500 lawyers practicing in them."[108]

But then the large-firm boom hit with a vengeance. Between 1978 and 1988, the number of firms with 200 or more lawyers increased from 15 to 115, and the number practicing in them increased tenfold (from about 3500 to more than 35,000).[109] An even larger increase occurred during the same period in the number of firms with more than 100 lawyers,[110] and these "megafirms" began to establish, for the first time in legal history, branch offices in key cities in and outside the United States.[111] These two trends, a dramatic increase in the number of lawyers practicing in large firms and the establishment of branch offices all over the country and world, probably did more to change the practice of law over roughly a decade than it had been changed by a multiplicity of factors over the preceding 100 years.

But what to do about it? Can—or, indeed, *should*—anything be done about it? Can we, for example, reverse the "weakening of the ties that once bound the individual members of a given firm to the firm itself, and made the movement of lawyers from one firm to another a rarity"?[112] What can be done, if anything, about the way "bureaucratization, impersonality, and pressure to generate business" have supplanted the former "sense of collegiality, institutional loyalty, and collective responsibility"?[113] Is there any way to shed the large firm experience of "a sense of anonymity and alienation, particularly when management decisions are made at a distance or a partner they have never met assigns tedious work in a case they have never heard of"?[114]

There is no question, as Professor Rhode put it, that "[p]rofit-driven priorities have had . . . unhappy consequences."[115] These "unhappy consequences" have included, *inter alia,* a severe reduction in the percentage of associates who make partner, pushing out senior practitioners who need or start to slow down for one reason or another, the previously noted workloads that leave little or no time for any personal life, and partners and associates who report increasing dissatisfaction with life in and outside the law. These proximate results of a money-centered law practice, particularly in the large-firm context, are undeniable. But what precisely can or should be done about them—whether by force of regulation or law or, more likely, through education and moral suasion—raises a series of tremendously complex questions.

The balance of this book will address these complex issues by focusing on choices we face as individuals and as a profession. We will consider "steps" the individual lawyer can take toward greater balance and, *ipso facto,* toward an increased fulfillment in the contemporary practice of law (chapter 4). We will also consider what role law schools, the organized bar, and the courts should play in bringing about the restoration and reform that is so badly needed (chapter 5).

Addressing the legal profession's contemporary needs, full as they are of complexity and nuance, will take our best minds—and hearts—and even then, success is not assured. Indeed, there are many who are cynical about the very idea of lawyers thinking beyond individual self-interest, let alone about what is consistent with the "common good." This attitude is reflected, for example, in the joke that asks why sharks, which routinely consume their own young, never eat lawyers. (Answer: "professional courtesy.")

Let's prove the cynics wrong. While we can never turn the clock back, let us strive as individuals and as a profession to reconnect with the more sustaining elements of our rich heritage. We are indebted, again, to Professor Glendon, who relates the story of Thomas Nelson Perkins of Boston's Ropes, Gray, Boyden & Perkins during the Great Depression. Having been advised that the firm would actually lose money unless its payroll expense was reduced, Perkins is said to have responded, "No young man is to be let go. The senior partners will take zero compensation."[116] Is it too much to hope that contemporary lawyers might once again see the immeasurable value of this kind of loyalty and commitment?

We turn our attention now from the problematic to the hopeful, from heavy facts and statistics to airier, more promising concepts and principles. In short, we turn our attention from what Professor Bogus called "the death of an honorable profession"[117] to the rekindling and restoration of a "high calling" that lawyers of all ages and stages of practice should be proud to embrace.

Notes

1. DONNA M. KILLOUGHEY, *Breaking Traditions: Work Alternatives for Lawyers, in* BREAKING TRADITIONS: WORK ALTERNATIVES FOR LAWYERS 3 (Donna M. Killoughey , ed., Am. Bar Ass'n, 1993).
2. *Id.*
3. ANTHONY T. KRONMAN, THE LOST LAWYER: FAILING IDEALS OF THE LEGAL PROFESSION 1–2 (1993).
4. *See* text in chapter 1 at note 54. According to Sol Linowitz, this was advice former Secretary of State and Nobel Prize winner Elihu Root described as "[a]bout half the practice of a decent lawyer."
5. DEBORAH L. RHODE, IN THE INTERESTS OF JUSTICE: REFORMING THE LEGAL PROFESSION 1 (2000). Rhode also directs the Keck Center on Legal Ethics and the Legal Profession at Stanford Law School, is a past-president of the Association of Am. Law Schools and chair of the ABA Commission on Women in the Profession.
6. *See* text in chapter 1 at notes 57–58.
7. *See* text in chapter 1 at note 59.
8. *See* text in chapter 1 at note 61.
9. *See* text in chapter 1 at notes 23–24.
10. RHODE, *supra* note 5, at 1, citing AM. LAWYER, *quoted in* MARC GALANTER & THOMAS PALAY, THE LAW FIRM AND THE PUBLIC GOOD 19, 38–39 (Robert A. Katzmann , ed., Brookings Institution, 1995). On this point, *see also* MARC GALANTER, *Predators and Parasites: Lawyer-Bashing and Civil Justice,* 28 GA. L. REV. 633, 670 (1994).
11. *Quoted in* SOL M. LINOWITZ (WITH MARTIN MAYER), THE BETRAYED PROFESSION: LAWYERING AT THE END OF THE TWENTIETH CENTURY 1 (1994) (emphasis added).
12. *Quoted in* RHODE, *supra* note 5, at 12.
13. WALT BACHMAN, LAW V. LIFE: WHAT LAWYERS ARE AFRAID TO SAY ABOUT THE LEGAL PROFESSION 110 (1995).
14. *Id.*
15. AMERICAN BAR ASS'N, THE PULSE OF THE PROFESSION 29 (November22, 2000).
16. *Id.*
17. *Id.*
18. MARY ANN GLENDON, A NATION UNDER LAWYERS 70 (1994).
19. *Id.*

20. *Id.*
21. *Id.*at 76.
22. *Id.* at 77.
23. LINOWITZ, *supra* note 11, at 107 (emphasis in original).
24. *Id.* at 107–08.
25. RHODE, *supra* note 5, at 9.
26. *Id.* at 9–10.
27. KILLOUGHEY, *supra* note 1, at 3.
28. RHODE, *supra* note 5, at 9–10.
29. KILLOUGHEY, *supra* note 1, at 3.
30. BENJAMIN SELLS, THE SOUL OF THE LAW: UNDERSTANDING LAWYERS AND THE LAW 63–64 (1994).
31. *Id.* at 64.
32. *Id.*
33. *Id.*
34. *Id.* at 76 (emphasis in original).
35. LAURENCE H. SILBERMAN, *Will Lawyering Strangle Democratic Capitalism?: A Retrospective*, 21 HARV. J.L. & PUB. POL'Y 607, 615 (1998).
36. RHODE, *supra* note 5, at 9–10.
37. KILLOUGHEY, *supra* note 1, at 3.
38. SELLS, *supra* note 30, at 63–64.
39. DICK DAHL, *The Trouble With Lawyers*, THE BOSTON GLOBE MAGAZINE, Apr. 14, 1996, at 26.
40. *Id.* at 28.
41. *Id.* at 27.
42. *Id.* at 29.
43. GLENDON, *supra* note 18, at 87.
44. MICHAEL TRAYNOR, *The Pursuit of Happiness*, 52 VAND. L. REV. 1025, 1027 (internal footnotes omitted)(emphasis in original).
45. RHODE, *supra* note 5, at 10.
46. *Id.*
47. PATRICK J. SCHILTZ, *On Being a Happy, Healthy, and Ethical Member of an Unhappy, Unhealthy, and Unethical Profession*, 52 VAND. L. REV. 871, 891 (May 1999).
48. *Id.*, citing a study by William Ross conducted in 1991. This is in accord with an ABA study conducted in 1990 in which 45 percent of private practitioners reported working "at least 1920 hours per year, and 16 percent billed 2400 or more hours."
49. *Id.*
50. *Id.*, citing ALTMAN WEIL PENSA, INC., THE 1996 SURVEY OF LAW FIRM ECONOMICS III-3 (1996).
51. *Quoted in Id.* at 892.

52. SELLS, *supra* note 30, at 99.
53. SCHILTZ, *supra* note 47, at 894 (emphasis in original).
54. *Id.* (internal footnote omitted).
55. CARL T. BOGUS, *The Death of an Honorable Profession*, 71 IND. L.J. 911, 925–26 (Fall 1996) (internal footnote omitted).
56. SILBERMAN, *supra* note 35, at 615.
57. JAMES J. ALFINI & JOSEPH N. VAN VOOREN, *Is There a Solution to the Problem of Lawyer Stress? The Law School Perspective*, 10 J.L. & HEALTH 61, 63 (1995-96).
58. DAVID A. KESSLER, *Professional Asphyxiation: Why the Legal Profession Is Gasping for Breath*, 10 GEO. J. LEGAL ETHICS 455, 466 (1997).
59. AMERICAN BAR ASS'N, AT THE BREAKING POINT: THE EMERGING CRISIS IN THE QUALITY OF LAWYERS' HEALTH AND LIVES, AND ITS IMPACT ON LAW FIRMS AND CLIENT SERVICES 3 (1991).
60. SCHILTZ, *supra* note 47, at 890, quoting a National Law Journal report.
61. WILLIAM H. REHNQUIST, *The Legal Profession Today*, 62 IND. L.J. 151, 155 (1987).
62. ABA, AT THE BREAKING POINT, *supra* note 59, at 11.
63. KRONMAN, *supra* note 3, at 378.
64. *Id.*
65. *Id.* at 379.
66. *Id.* at 380.
67. *Quoted in* DAHL, *supra* note 39, at 32.
68. *Id.*
69. WALT BACHMAN, LAW V. LIFE: WHAT LAWYERS ARE AFRAID TO SAY ABOUT THE LEGAL PROFESSION (1995). Although this small but rich account of one bright, well-educated lawyer's experience did not receive wide enough circulation to start a movement, Bachman's book was the first of a series of articles and books by those who tried large-firm practice and found it wanting. For others, *see* text at notes 72–89.
70. *See* note 71 in chapter 1.
71. BACHMAN, *supra* note 69, at 6.
72. JONATHAN FOREMAN, *My Life as an Associate*, CITY JOURNAL (Winter 1997) at 88.
73. *Id.*
74. *Id.* at 89.
75. *Id.* at 89–90.
76. *Id.* at 91.
77. *Id.*
78. *Id.* at 92.
79. CAMERON STRACHER, DOUBLE BILLING: A YOUNG LAWYER'S TALE OF GREED, SEX, LIES, AND THE PURSUIT OF A SWIVEL CHAIR (1998).

80. CAMERON STRACHER, *Show Me the Misery,* WALL ST. J., Mar. 6, 2000, at A31.
81. STRACHER, *supra* note 79, at 2, 11. There were 97 partners and 205 associates in the New York office when Stracher joined the firm, plus 20 lawyers in their Los Angeles office and 30 lawyers in smaller offices in Paris, London, Brussels, and Budapest.
82. *Id.* at 19.
83. *Id.* at 58–59.
84. STRACHER, *supra* note 80.
85. *Id.*
86. *Id.*
87. STRACHER, *supra* note 79, at 212.
88. *Id.* at 213.
89. *Id.* at 226.
90. SCHILTZ, *supra* note 47, at 892.
91. *Id.* at 892–93 (internal footnotes omitted).
92. *Id.* at 893 (internal footnotes omitted).
93. RHODE, *supra* note 5, at 34.
94. CHRIS KLEIN, *Big-Firm Partners: Profession Sinking,* NAT'L L.J., May 26, 1997, at A1.
95. *Id.*
96. *Id.*
97. *Id.*
98. RICHARD B. SCHMITT, FROM CASH TO TRAVEL, *New Lures for Burned-Out Lawyers,* WALL ST. J., Feb. 2, 1999, at B1.
99. ABA, *supra* note 15, at 26.
100. *Id.* at 25 (emphasis added).
101. *Id.* at 26.
102. *Id.*
103. *Id.*
104. *Id.* at 25.
105. LINOWITZ, *supra* note 11, at 27.
106. BOGUS, *supra* note 55, at 923.
107. LINOWITZ, *supra* note 11, at 27–28.
108. KRONMAN, *supra* note 3, at 274.
109. *Id.*
110. *Id.*
111. *Id.*, citing "[a] detailed study of law firm growth by Marc Galanter and Thomas Palay, resulting in what Galanter and Palay call "the genuine multicity firm."
112. *Id.* at 277.
113. RHODE, *supra* note 5, at 34.
114. *Id.*
115. *Id.* at 35.
116. GLENDON, *supra* note 18, at 21.
117. BOGUS, *supra* note 55.

Part Two

Where Do We Go From Here?

CHAPTER 4

Twelve Steps Toward Fulfillment in the Practice of Law

Remedies for the professionwide ills identified in Part I fall in two broad categories: (1) those based on individual choices, and (2) systemic initiatives and reforms. This chapter focuses on the former, that is, on life and career decisions the individual lawyer can make to enhance professional fulfillment. Chapter 5 will address systemic initiatives and reforms in legal education, law firms, the organized bar, and the courts.

This chapter is organized, only partly with tongue in cheek, as the world's first 12-step program for lawyers.[1] Although there is nothing magic about the delineation or order of the recommended "steps," there has been an intentional blending of the professional and the personal. Keeping that in mind, the 12 steps toward greater fulfillment in the practice of law—and in life generally—are:

- Step 1. Face the facts.
- Step 2. Establish clear priorities.
- Step 3. Develop and practice good time management.
- Step 4. Implement healthy lifestyle practices.
- Step 5. Live *beneath* your means.
- Step 6. Don't let technology control your life.
- Step 7. Care about character—and conduct yourself accordingly.
- Step 8. "Just say no" to some clients.
- Step 9. Stay emotionally healthy.
- Step 10. Embrace law as a "high calling."

- Step 11. Be generous with your time and money.
- Step 12. Pace yourself for a marathon.

Whether you are a law student making initial career decisions, an associate or partner in mid-career, or a senior practitioner, these 12 steps will help you avoid—and, if need be, reverse—the troubling trends discussed in preceding chapters. Law professors, judges, and others in close working or personal relationships with lawyers may also find these recommendations useful.

Several assumptions underlie the recommended steps. First, there has been an attempt, as noted, to integrate the strictly *professional* with more *personal* goals and values. Although properly kept separate and distinct in other contexts, when work takes as much of our life energies as does the contemporary practice of law, the professional and personal dimensions of our lives are in unavoidable tension. Facing this tension head on, the intent has been to develop "steps" that will enhance our fulfillment not only professionally but also on a deeper personal level.

The second assumption has been the utility of the simple and straightforward over the more complex, where possible. On one level, of course, the problems facing the legal profession are mind-bendingly complex, as indeed are the problems facing contemporary society generally. Some effort has been made to acknowledge relevant complexities, nuances, and caveats in preceding chapters. On the other hand, as theologian Richard John Neuhaus has reminded us, we on occasion find "simplicity on the other side of complexity." Many of the readers will have enjoyed introductory courses taught by brilliant professors who know more about their subjects than most would ever care to hear, but could nevertheless communicate broad concepts in a lucid, simple, and compelling manner. This is the simplicity on the other side of complexity for which we strive.

The third assumption or organizing principle has been the need to balance objective data and recommendations on the one hand, with more subjective "steps" on the other. The observation that honestly billing more than 1800 or 1900 hours per year will seriously impinge on one's ability to be a sufficiently present parent or an available friend or a volunteer in the community or even a happy person—whether you agree with it or not—is more or less an objective one. The same is true of specific time-management and minimal-exercise recommendations, as well as cautions about intrusive technology that never allows the relief from work everyone needs. On the other hand, exhortations to make significant relationships a priority, to care about character, to embrace law as a "high calling," and to pay attention to emotional health all tend toward the attitudinal and subjective. Although some hyper-rational lawyers may have difficulty with the latter recommendations, dismissing them as too "touchy-feely," this does not make the subjective any less important. This is true, as University of Chicago Professor (of English) Richard M. Weaver urged in his book of the same title, because "ideas have consequences."[2]

As we have seen, the concept of law as a public service "calling" led prior generations of lawyers to volunteer countless hours to their communities, to worthy organizations and causes, and to clients unable to pay their fees. Not surprisingly, public respect for lawyers and professional "fulfillment" followed what began essentially as an idea, or a series of ideas, about what it meant to be a lawyer. Conversely, as cynicism about the higher purposes of law—and *the idea* in some quarters that making money is sufficient *raison d'etre* for the profession—have taken hold, public approval and lawyer happiness appear to have fallen. As you reflect on the following "12-step program for lawyers," keep in mind that subjective attitudes and abstract ideas often precede objective changes in conduct. That is why, to successfully counter contemporary problems and trends, we must address both.

Step 1. Face the facts

Every 12-step program begins with an exhortation to those in the targeted group to acknowledge their need. "My name is John, and I am an alcoholic (or I am addicted to sex or food or some other habit or compulsion)." In current context, perhaps one would say, "I am a lawyer who went to law school (or began practice) with high ideals, intentions to live a balanced life, and all that, but now. . . . "

Part I (chapters 1 through 3) addressed survey data, anecdotal evidence, and expert opinion that collectively suggest troubling trends in the legal profession. Some commentators, particularly those writing from the academy, see the profession as dying, as "on the edge of chaos,"[3] or otherwise as being in extremis. Others, particularly older practitioners, lament that the profession they have proudly served has become an increasingly unprincipled, dollar-driven business;[4] express concern over decreases in collegiality, civility and "professionalism";

worry about the precipitous decline in public respect; and/or simply note that they are working more but enjoying it less.

These are the professionwide "facts," but they are *not* primarily the facts we are being invited to face in Step 1. Here we are being asked to make a more personal assessment. How am I doing in light of my own values, standards, and priorities? Have they changed? Am I pleased with the balance in my professional and personal life? Are my priorities, as evidenced by how I spend my time week in and week out, consistent with any principles, dreams, or ideals I once brought to the table? Am I a professional who treats colleagues—and opponents—with civility and respect? Or we might ask, if I were on trial for being a nice person, or a successful parent, or a good citizen, or [insert what quality or virtue *you* hope to reflect], would there be enough evidence to convict me?

The surveys and studies reported in Chapter 2 clearly indicate less satisfaction and more dysfunction in the practicing bar. A sizeable minority describes itself as dissatisfied to the point that they do not plan to practice law until retirement. In several surveys a majority would recommend against one of their own children following in their professional footsteps. And a not-insignificant minority is so "miserable" they are currently being treated for clinical depression or have even been contemplating suicide.

It is hoped these more distressing reports do not describe a large percentage of the readers of this book, but be honest: If you were to give yourself a "happiness check," on a one-to-ten scale, where are you? How does that compare to three years ago or five years ago? Or, for that matter, to when you were in college or law school or got married or had your first child? Are you emotionally healthy? Are you satisfied with the key relationships in your life? When you look back on these years, will you be pleased with your priorities—as evidenced by how you *actually* spent your time—or will you regret not having spent more time with your family and close friends? In short, do you feel good about where you are professionally and personally and where your life appears to be going? Let honesty be the rule here.

We each must face these facts, and not just once but on a regular basis, if our lives are to remain balanced and on course. Lawyers who do not ask these kinds of questions, who fail to engage in periodic introspection, are more likely to experience what Dr. Benjamin Sells has described as "the lingering feeling of emptiness despite material success."[5] Others will realize at some point that the stress in their life has grown intolerable, that in Judge Silberman's words they "hate what the practice of law has become,"[6] or that their use of alcohol or other substances has moved into the danger zone.

It would be naive, of course, to suggest that all trouble can be avoided, or happiness assured, by any simple exercise. However, by honestly and openly asking the right questions, we increase our chances—that is, we take the first step—toward a balanced, fulfilling professional life.

Step 2. Establish clear priorities

Let us continue in this realistic and honest vein. In the very best of times practicing law has been a challenging, time-consuming, and often difficult undertaking. The origins of the maxim about the law as a "jealous mistress" are lost in history, but it goes back at least to the 1950s when a majority of lawyers were solo practitioners or had one or two partners. And it certainly predates the era of billable-hour requirements, the geometric increase in large-firm practice, young lawyers who require six-figure incomes to pay off five- or even six-figure educational debts; and other stressors of more recent origin.

Although lawyers in prior generations worked hard, and on occasion were consumed by their work, broad dissatisfaction with the profession was simply not an issue. Law has never been a nine-to-five job, but Jonathan Foreman's description of associates in his large New York firm as "wage slaves"[7] would have almost certainly fallen on deaf ears even as recently as the 1970s. And somehow the lawyers in these earlier generations still found time to serve their communities, mentor younger colleagues, be sociable with one another, and do an impressive amount of *pro bono* work.

What has changed? Why does it seem so excruciatingly difficult today to engage in all these laudable professional and civic activities—not to mention to find time and emotional energy for family and friends, for exercise and other "healthy lifestyle practices," or every now and then, just to "chill out"?

One major reason for the change, seldom mentioned in the laments on lost balance, is the larger-than-law demographic shift, beginning in earnest in the 1960s, from one- to two-wage-earner families. Indeed, the jealous *mistress* metaphor fit, in part, because most of the lawyers were men—and, more pertinent to the point at hand, most had non-working wives devoting time and talent to family and their lives' personal dimensions. Men had a more limited concept of their parental role as primarily "to put food on the table," and most enjoyed the free services of a stay-at-home mom who took care of responsibilities most contemporary couples now share. Indeed, this fundamental demographic shift is so significant and pervasive that we are almost "comparing apples to oranges" when we look to earlier generations of lawyers for inspiration or guidance.

Whether single or married and, if married with children, whether one or two of the parents work outside the home, there is a widespread sense today that there is never enough time. And that is precisely why it is crucial to establish clear priorities. As someone once quipped, "If you don't know where you're going, any road will take you there." We must know at least where we *want* to go with our professional and personal lives—and prioritize our time accordingly.

Brian Warnock, an Arizona lawyer and real-estate developer, learned this lesson in what my country-bred grandfather would have called "the hard way." Giving what is essentially a personal testimonial, Warnock began his contribution to the ABA's 1993 publication, *Breaking Traditions: Work Alternatives for Lawyers*, with an evocative question. "What do you do when you wake up one day," he asks, "and realize that your priorities have been distorted for more than 20 years?"[8]

Warnock's story, an increasingly familiar one, might on one level be described as "too much of a good thing." Raised by "Depression-era parents" who instilled in him the kind of work ethic that often leads to material success but can also lead to unhealthy workaholism, Warnock's wake-up call came in the form of "three cataclysmic events" in a single year: His partner in the development company had a nervous breakdown, his wife of 16 years and the mother of his two children was diagnosed with cancer, and the real estate market in which he was heavily invested began what was to become "its tremendous plummet."[9]

Reminiscent of Aleksandr Solzhenitsyn's "bless the prison" comment in *The Gulag Archipelago*, Warnock elected to learn and grow from these life-shaking events. Beginning with "a concerted program to get [his] priorities in order," he quickly realized that while he was working 12-plus hours a day, six or seven days a week, his daughters and wife had been growing and developing largely without him. "I felt a little like Rip Van Winkle," Warnock reports. "Where had the years gone since I rocked them to sleep?"[10]

Brian Warnock is one of the lucky ones. He "woke up" after only 20 years, before it was too late to rekindle relationships with the family he always considered, at least in the abstract, to be the primary reason he was working so long and so hard. Others are less lucky because, as San Francisco lawyer Michael Traynor reflected toward the end of his career, the child-raising years slip away in a blur if we are not careful. Writing in the *Vanderbilt Law Review* in 1999 (when he was in his late 60s), Traynor gave some retrospective advice every parent should heed:

> I will emphasize that the years with your children fly by in an instant, that they and time with them are precious, and that I wish I had spent more. Whenever you can, tell the god of money and the god of ambition, who is no less voracious, that you and your kids are going to fly a kite or build a snowman.[11]

The bottom line: to avoid later-life regrets, realize *now* that the time you spend with your children will be remembered as "precious"—and as far more valuable than more money or any temporary career achievement you may have to forego. Make spending time with your family a top priority, and be sure your daily and weekly schedules reflect it.

This does not mean that lawyers, with or without children, should not be prepared to work very hard. It simply means that, if we aim to live balanced lives, lines must be drawn beyond which we are not willing to go, at least not on a regular basis. In other words, living a balanced life—in which quality time is regularly saved for our families and other close relationships—should itself become one of our top priorities. And when people or pressures repeatedly push us in a contrary direction, we must learn to say politely but firmly, "Sorry, that part of me is not for sale." Or words to that effect.

Again, let us stay realistic and honest: Having enough money is important, and as a repairman once responded when I questioned his bill, "Life ain't cheap." In fact, let us go a step further and agree that making enough money should be one of our "clearly established priorities." However, the proper priority in a balanced life that should be given to making *enough* money must not become a license for workaholism or what one commentator called a "money-centered world view." Money is a means to an end. If balance and happiness are among our life goals, we must be vigilant not to allow money to become an end in itself.[12]

Ronald H. Kessel, then–Managing Partner of Palmer & Dodge in Boston, made this point at the previously noted meeting of the

Women's Bar Association of Massachusetts where "The Misery Factor" was the appointed topic for discussion. Illustrating perhaps the wisdom in Voltaire's quip that "common sense is not so common," Kessel counseled those present "to be prepared to make less. It's not the end of the world. You don't have to make more and more money at the price of being miserable."[13]

Harvard Law Professor Alan Dershowitz makes related points in *Letters to a Young Lawyer*,[14] a quick but engaging read for lawyers of any age. In a three-page reflection titled "Don't Limit Your Options By Making a Lot of Money," Professor Dershowitz recounts friends and former students who have turned down jobs they had always wanted because they "can't afford" the reduced income.[15] Dershowitz points to "the irony . . . that [those] who turned down judgeships or other dream jobs were richer when they had less money and poorer when they had more."[16]

"Money matters, and there's nothing wrong with wanting to live a comfortable, even financially independent life," Professor Dershowitz concedes.[17] But, like the wealthiest people at his family's preferred vacation spot who "tend to have the shortest vacations, because every day away from *their* work costs them more money than the rest of us," Dershowitz is absolutely correct that "too many rich people . . . end up living financially *dependent* lives."[17] And he is also correct that "[w]hen money enslaves rather than liberates, something is wrong."[18] Badly wrong.

Law students looking at career options should be especially careful, as Professor Patrick J. Schiltz put it, not to permit themselves "to be purchased at auction like a prize hog at the county fair. Do not choose one law firm over another because of a $3,000 difference in starting salaries."[19] Rather, "make it clear to prospective employers that salary is only one of many factors you will consider in choosing a law firm."[20] Of course, you should expect to work very hard, and sometimes this will require "long hours at the office (and terrifically long hours when you have a case about to try or a deal about to close)."[21] But "[t]hat said, you should at least signal a prospective employer that, while you intend to work hard and be successful, you also intend to do more with your life than rack up billable hours. You can and should let prospective employers know you do not intend to permit work to consume your life and that you are willing to sacrifice some money in order to have a life outside the office."[22]

Brian Warnock, Michael Traynor, and Ronald Kessel are three successful lawyers who would certainly agree; each has learned the importance of what we are here calling "Step 2." They learned that, if we are to realize professional fulfillment, we must establish—and unequivocally live by—clear priorities. They learned, in other words, the importance of what some of our parents correctly described as "putting first things first." They learned, to go right to the bottom line, that if we hope to be happy, establishing clear priorities is a must.

Step 3. Develop and practice good time management

Turning our attention from somewhat subjective values and priorities, the more pragmatically inclined will be pleased to note that our next step—developing and practicing good time management—is about as practical as it gets. Here, we simply agree that *whatever* time we spend on our work should be arranged for maximum productivity.

In the "olden days," this was simply referred to as being efficient or "well organized." Somewhere along the way, as in so many areas, experts emerged in what came to be called "time management." Like experts in organizing closets or garages, personal trainers, and the like, some experts in time management can be quite helpful, even if they essentially offer common-sense solutions that many of our predecessors discovered instinctively or by trial and error.

I thought recently of this phenomenon—the appearance of "experts" in areas formerly left to individual initiative—when a close friend, who is married to a successful doctor, retained a personal-finances expert. After paying him thousands of dollars, Dr. So-And-So made two stunningly insightful recommendations: (1) when borrowing to purchase a new car or boat or whatever, at some point plan to pay more than just the interest on the loan; and (2) try to keep spending, including repayment of accumulated debt, somewhere below all available income. ("That will be $5,000, please.")

This example is not offered to broadly disparage time-management or other experts. Some are very good and, in fact, several of their books and articles will be heartily recommended. However, keep in mind that there are certain basic organizational insights and habits, formerly thought to be within lay expertise, that you can begin to apply immediately.

One book that is full of practical insights on how to use time more efficiently is Alec Mackenzie's *The Time Trap.*[23] First published in

1990 by the American Management Association, its widespread appeal is evidenced by the thousands of copies that continue to be sold each year. Lawyers will find Mackenzie's discussion of the top 20 "time wasters" particularly pertinent and helpful. According to the author, the key impediments to our efficiency at work are:[24]

1. Management by Crisis
2. Telephone Interruptions
3. Inadequate Planning
4. Attempting Too Much
5. Drop-in Visitors
6. Ineffective Delegation
7. Personal Disorganization
8. Lack of Self-Discipline
9. Inability to Say "No"
10. Procrastination
11. Meetings
12. Paperwork
13. Unfinished Tasks
14. Inadequate Staff
15. Socializing
16. Confused Authority
17. Poor Communication
18. Inadequate Controls
19. Incomplete Information
20. Travel

Of course, certain points in any general discussion of time management will be more applicable to law practice than others, but Mackenzie's recommendations are a must read for any lawyer—from the "organizational challenged" to those for whom efficiency and organization come more naturally.

In addition to insights gleaned from time-management experts, whether by reading their books and articles or retaining one, there are at least five areas in which many lawyers could begin to make significant progress simply by paying closer attention. They are: (1) better planning; (2) minimizing interruptions (by phone or in person); (3) more careful scheduling/planning of meetings; (4) mastering the paper flow; and (5) more thoughtful and efficient delegation. Although not intended as a substitute for more in-depth analysis by the experts, it is hoped that even cursory discussion of these "time wasters" will convince the reader of the efficacy and potential of what we are here calling "Step 3."

In her contribution to the ABA's 1997 publication *Living with the Law: Strategies to Avoid Burnout and Create Balance*, time-management expert Margaret S. Spencer emphasizes the central importance of better planning. Spencer graduated from Princeton University and Stanford Law School, completed a federal appellate clerkship, and practiced for six years in the litigation and energy groups of a major D.C. law firm before turning her considerable intelligence and talents to helping lawyers get better organized. At the heart of the advice she gives, as president of Spencer Consulting, is a foundational recommendation that lawyers spend more time in daily planning.

"Preparing and following a daily, written, prioritized 'to-do' list is the single most powerful time-management technique," Spencer has concluded.[25] Otherwise, "you end up working on whatever project pops into your mind first, or whatever project is most noticeable on your desk, rather than a project you have consciously decided is the most important."[26] Taking a step back from what has been called "the tyranny of the urgent" to plan how our limited time *should* be spent is also "the best way to minimize the possibility a task will be overlooked. In other words, a good to-do list helps you see the forest *and* the trees."[27]

Spencer suggests six steps toward creation and maintenance of an effective to-do list. Although there is nothing sacrosanct about the individual steps, and some may find them too detailed or cumbersome, there is also much substance in her detailed recommendations, and those with busy practices may want to appropriate most or all of them.

"First," Spencer counsels every busy lawyer, "make a written list of all the projects and tasks that you 'must' do, in the order that they come to mind, leaving a wide margin on the left-hand side of the paper [or PDA screen]. . . . List each project in discrete sections that can be completed in an hour or less. For example, instead of listing 'prepare memorandum of points and authorities,' write something like 'legal research for memo—bias issue'. . . ,'draft first section of memo,' and so on. Cutting each project into bite-sized chunks gives a clearer picture of the work to be done, helps you schedule your work realistically . . . [and] makes it a less likely target for procrastination."[28]

"Second, go through this general list, assigning each project a priority level of A, B, C, or D, and writing the letter *in pencil* in the left-hand margin."[29] Spencer explains:

> A-level tasks are those that are both urgent and important (i.e., tasks that must be completed within the next few days to avoid serious negative consequences), such as drafting direct examination questions for a trial set for next week. B-level tasks are important but not urgent (i.e,, tasks that must be completed at some point beyond the next few days to avoid serious negative consequences), such as planning a general litigation strategy for a new case. C-level tasks are those minor matters that are urgent but not particularly important (i.e., tasks that, if not completed at some point in the

very near future, would yield minor negative consequences), such as responding to an invitation to a function in which you are not particularly interested. D-level tasks are neither urgent nor important (i.e,, tasks that can be left undone indefinitely with only minor negative consequences), such as going through your address files to delete the names of people with whom you are no longer in contact.[30]

Author's note: whether one utilizes these precise categories (or even, for that matter, these six steps) is less important than that written, prioritized planning become an essential part of the daily work routine.

"Third," Spencer continues, "within each priority category, number each task (again, in the left margin and in pencil) according to its relative importance and the order in which logic requires the task to be done."[31] Spencer notes that this will help you focus, for example, on the need to delegate a portion of a project that may be a lower priority for you, but that needs prompt attention by someone in order for the overall project to be completed on time. In any event, at the conclusion of this step, "each item on your list will have a unique letter and number combination, such as A1, B1, and so forth."[32]

Fourth, from this general list, prepare a separate, shorter written list, which will constitute your daily to-do list. Include only those tasks that you realistically think you can complete that day, keeping in mind other commitments such as appointments and meetings."[33]

The fifth step is to start with project A1, and—as far as possible given the nature of your practice—*stay with it until it is finished. Continue with A2, A3, and so on, checking off each task as you complete it, until you finish all the A-level tasks."*[34]

Next we proceed with the B-level tasks, again *sticking with each task until it is done.* C-level projects, which are usually such tasks as dictating a letter, returning a phone call, or paying a bill, can be done during the transition time between the important projects, or during those times (such as just after lunch) when you know you are at your least productive."[35]

Spencer is a realist, recognizing that to-do lists will frequently have to be amended as "new tasks" or even "emergencies" come up. Rather than becoming unfocused and sidetracked by the unexpected, however, she counsels lawyers to plug the unplanned for work in *according to the priority it objectively deserves.* That which is really an emergency, for example, would likely be given an A1 priority as opposed to unexpected work that would have been given a lower priority had you known about it in advance. Work should not be elevated to a higher priority simply because it caught you by surprise.

Finally, "[a]s the sixth and last step, at the end of the day (or whenever you make your next to-do list), go back to your general list, cross off all the tasks you completed that day, add whatever new tasks arose that day, reprioritize tasks as necessary, and make a new daily to-do list according to the steps previously described."[36]

Your author has been using a streamlined version of Margaret Spencer's prioritized to-do list for many years, and highly recommends it. As has been noted, it is not the precise way it is created or used that makes having a "daily plan" such a valuable time management tool. Rather, it is the fact that we are able, daily, to step back from the deluge of demands and pressures and decide which work deserves our limited time and energy.

My own daily and weekly planning includes elements and nuances some readers may find useful. First, I have daily plans (on 8 1/2-by-11-inch lined paper) for two to three weeks ahead at any given time. Of course, they are skeletal two to three weeks out and must be amended as new appointments or work arise. Every Thursday or Friday, usually at the end of the day once it quiets down, I go through a week-at-a-glance calendar one legal publisher provides and create another week (the third week out) of daily plans. One of the benefits of looking several weeks ahead is that it frequently points to preparatory work (or errands or calls) that need to be noted for action a week or two earlier.

Centered at the top of each daily plan I write and underline the day and date. On the left side I record, in red ink, any appointment, engagement, or event—basically any time I am expected to be somewhere, including in chambers, at a particular time. Below that I record, in blue ink, the files, projects, and other "action items" on which I plan to work that day. About half-way down the sheet I write and underline "Calls," and then record them in pencil (with numbers, an added efficiency you will learn to appreciate). Finally, on the right side of the sheet I record any errands I hope to run or things I need to remember to do when I get home. (I also keep a 3-by-5 card in my shirt pocket for errands and at-home entries. As long as I write it down on my daily plan or the 3-by-5 card, I can relax and usually avoid unwelcome "surprises.")

One feature of my approach on which Ms. Spencer is silent, but that I strongly recommend, is the inclusion of personal and work-related to-do items on a single daily plan. For example, if one of my children has an athletic or other event, it goes in red. If I have agreed to write a letter of recommendation for a family friend, it goes in blue. Likewise, personal phone calls and errands are entered on a single daily plan. There is just one of each of us, with limited hours and energy to give, and I find that this kind of integration of professional life and equally important personal obligations is essential to a sense of being "successful" at either.

Several other brief suggestions regarding planning, in no particular order:

1. Keep a master annual calendar of key birthdays of family and friends, and enter them in your new calendar each year—both on the day of and sufficiently ahead to send a gift or card.
2. Always carry a 3-by-5 card and a pen, even on weekends, so you can make a note of things that come to mind (and then forget them), note errands and be more efficient in running them, and so on.
3. Keep a separate list of the work you have assigned to others (their abbreviated "to-do list"), and mark items off as they are completed. (This has the double benefit of taking those items off *your* list and making you a more efficient supervisor.)
4. At the end of each day, transfer any remaining items to tomorrow's daily plan.
5. Then go home, feel satisfied about a good day's work, and resist any nagging thought that you should have done more. If you have planned well and worked efficiently for the appointed time, there is little constructive about these worrisome thoughts. You have worked enough.

Making progress on the second and third time wasters—interruptions and meetings—also requires a clear, prioritized plan for our work. Only then can a reasoned decision be made about whether to take the phone call, agree to meet, delegate to an administrative assistant or associate, and so forth. In other words, without a daily plan we have no way of evaluating whether the unexpected claim on our time advances the "big picture" ball, or is a digression to be postponed or avoided altogether. Although this is a simple concept with which it is hard to disagree, it is frequently neglected in actual practice.

As every time-management expert will confirm, how we handle telephone calls is of tremendous importance. This includes whether and when to accept calls, how best to screen calls, by whom and when calls are returned, and how much time we spend on a particular call. While answers to these questions are to some degree a matter of personal style and preference, there are inherent efficiencies to keep clearly in mind as we determine what works best for us.

The principal efficiency enhancer in regard to telephone calls is simple: To the extent possible, avoid interruptions while working on priority projects during the most productive period of your day. This will require a good call-screening system, preferably by a person rather than a machine, and a healthy measure of diplomacy. Some calls have to be taken, of course, but you may be surprised how few that turns out to be. And for those clients or others who are unreasonably offended by your eminently reasonable efforts to use time more wisely, perhaps you should skip directly to Step 8 ("Just say no" to some clients)!

The importance of having a good administrative assistant, someone who projects warmth and competence *and* can efficiently handle what would otherwise become interruptions, cannot be overemphasized. If you have this kind of working relationship already, be thankful. And be sure to show it financially and by regular, thoughtful expressions of personal gratitude. If not, you should make finding and training a good administrative assistant one of your "A1" priorities.

Once it is determined which interruptions should be blocked, whether they present by phone or in person, as many as possible should be handled by your administrative assistant or an associate. ("Ms. Lawyer is not available right now. Could I help you?") Others, like the talkative coworker or friend, can be dealt with during what you decide is properly "downtime." Some calls will have to be returned personally, but if you know the subject of the inquiry in advance—something a well-trained administrative assistant will find out and can give you, frequently with a proposed response—you can also significantly reduce the time you spend on the *necessary* calls. And you can save all this time and prevent many concentration-breaking interruptions without offending or appearing to be less "available," at least to those callers or erstwhile visitors who are themselves reasonable.

Like all "best-laid plans," even the most efficient approach to telephone calls will not prevent a certain amount of time and energy loss playing "phone tag." However, as Margaret Spencer observes, several small steps will go a long way toward reducing this residual annoyance. First, return calls as promptly as you can, consistent with the previously recommended approach—not days later, for example. Second, if you know what the call was about and can leave a message with the likely answer, there may be no need for a follow-up call. Third, if you jot down or otherwise have a written response in hand, you will probably convey it more efficiently, whether you are speaking to a person or a machine. Fourth, if you must leave a message requesting a return call, "include the specific time or times you are most likely to be available [to receive it]."[37]

As with interruptions generally, we can only determine whether it is advisable to set up or attend a meeting if we first have a clear, prioritized plan for our daily work. The plan is the big picture; meetings are details that only make good sense from a time-management perspective if they fit into it.

Many meetings are scheduled unnecessarily, that is, the perceived need for the meeting could be satisfied, for example, by letter or a 20-minute conference call. Some meetings are planned prematurely, before the issues at hand are sufficiently ripe to allow for their efficient resolution. Even meetings that are properly scheduled often lack a clearly defined agenda, which almost always results in more time being spent on nonessential tangents than is justified or reasonable.

A word to the wise before you set up or agree to attend a meeting: Decide that its purpose is consistent with your own work plan. Assuming it is, ask yourself whether a meeting is really necessary, who should attend, and whether the timing is right. Finally, if preliminary analysis yields a green light, either prepare a clearly defined agenda for the meeting, or insist that someone else prepare one—and then stick to it.

A fourth area in which many lawyers could save considerable time is in the handling and processing of "the plethora of paper that continually crosses [our] desks."[38] The key principles here are: (1) touch the paper the minimum number of times (where possible, just once); (2) read and deal with "the plethora of paper" in a time and manner consistent with your written daily plan, not allowing paper itself to become an inefficient interruption; and (3) whatever you do, do not get buried in it.

The first step toward time efficiency in handling paper is deciding how to sort it, and a close second step is determining when to review and deal with it. Obviously if you are working on a motion and a relevant pleading comes in, the answer to the latter question is right now. On the other hand, you should not allow yourself to be drawn into a memorandum in a B- or C- priority project during a time you have set aside for more pressing work. Yes, this is not rocket science, but it is astounding how often simple insights like this are overlooked in actual practice.

Margaret Spencer suggests sorting papers initially into three categories: "(1) to file, (2) to read, and (3) administrative."[39] There may be different or additional categories that work better for you, of course. Whatever categories you choose for initial sorting, efficiency lies in selecting the right time or times to attack the paper monster and then spending the least possible time on each item.

Spencer encourages lawyers to "[r]esist the temptation to spend more than a few seconds with any item until you have gone through the entire pile."[40] Like many rules there are exceptions to this one, but it is generally good advice. In any event, the idea is to go through "the daily deluge"[41] quickly, throwing away (or preferably, putting in a recycling bin) what we do not need to keep, and sorting the rest according to time sensitivity and our own preexisting priorities.

We have all seen lawyers' desks covered with clutter, and indeed there will be readers of this book, some of whom are very fine lawyers, who fall in that category. Perhaps it is the author's Germanic brain that craves order and cannot work well amongst clutter, but I will offer this advice to all: You will save time and *feel* more caught up and organized, if you avoid even *the appearance* of being buried in paper work.

A fifth time waster afflicting many lawyers is insufficient attention given to how and when to delegate. The value of a good administrative assistant, who becomes in highest form almost an alter ego, has been extolled. Similar praise and commendation can be given, from a time-management perspective alone, to well-trained paralegals.

For those with the luxury of associates (or partners) to whom work can be delegated, the same principles apply. Conversely, if "you live by the rule that the way to get things done right is to do them yourself," as Dr. Amiram Elwork put it in *Stress Management for Lawyers: How to Increase Personal and Professional Satisfaction in the Law,*[42] get over it. The time and energy you alone have to give can and will soon run out. What you can accomplish by the thoughtful and efficient delegation to others is significantly less limited.

Dr. Elwork is absolutely correct that an inability to delegate efficiently "can be a most debilitating and time wasting habit."[43] He is also correct that if we "hire the right people, [are] clear in [our] instructions, and create a supportive psychological environment" we are far better off "liv[ing] by a different rule: anything that can be done by others should be done by them."[44]

The bottom line: Those who learn to delegate effectively will free up many of their own hours and see their productivity significantly rise. Who, exercising reasonable judgment, would decline that kind of bargain?

It is hoped that even this cursory discussion of these five areas—planning, interruptions (by telephone and otherwise), meetings, managing paper, and delegating—will whet the reader's appetite for more in-depth information. There is much that is promising and hopeful in what has come to be called "time management," and there are an increasing number of experts available to help. But whether the individual lawyer relies on expert advice or goes it alone, arranging our limited time for maximum productivity is an important step toward fulfillment in the contemporary practice.

Step 4. Implement healthy lifestyle practices

In considering how to broach this subject I find myself feeling like a scolding parent. "Eat your peas," I hear my father saying sternly, or "Go outside and play." And, as best I can recall almost a half-century later, that approach did not work particularly well when I was on the receiving end.

I believe it was the North Carolina Bar Association's report of a 1989 study that first used the phrase "healthy lifestyle practices." Reporting in 1991 on a statewide survey distributed by its Quality of Life Task Force two years earlier, the authors noted a positive correlation between lawyers who self-reported a sense of "subjective well-being" and those who engaged in certain habits or practices the reporters deemed "healthy."

The reader will probably not be surprised that "regular exercise" was the first healthy practice noted (based on the highest correlation with those reporting "subjective well-being"), but may find the somewhat eclectic list that followed more noteworthy. According to the North Carolina Bar Association report, the other regular practices that were predictors of contentment or "well-being" (in order of importance) were: attending religious services, personal prayer, having hobbies, engaging in outdoor recreation, pleasure reading, and taking *weeks* of vacation. In a word, the lawyers with other serious interests—those who successfully resisted the "all work and no play" syndrome—also considered themselves the happiest.

Of course, exercise is a "no-brainer." We all know we need it, and every medical report on exercise extols its positive effects on health and longevity. And yet, what scant data there is suggests that about "[h]alf of lawyers do *not* exercise regularly."[45]

Margaret S. Spencer, the lawyer-turned-time-management expert cited in the previous "step," regards exercise as "a necessary time commitment" on a par with the many office-bound tasks we have to juggle.[46] Indeed, as Spencer observed, the more demands and pressure we face, the greater need we have for the stress-relieving effects of a good workout:

> Being in good physical shape can make it much easier to handle these periods of extreme stress and can also make you feel better and more energetic during periods of normal stress. You can *always* make time to exercise once you realize that a moderate amount . . . of vigorous, aerobic exercise gives you so much energy that it more than compensates for the time you spend exercising.[47]

Lawyers who already exercise will affirm its paradoxical time-expanding qualities, partly due to the calming effect of the endorphins it dispatches to our tired and overworked brains. But even if this were not the case, there is simply no excuse for anyone who cares about their health not to *make time* for regular exercise.

As to the beneficial effects of religious or spiritual practices, the reader will find further support for this observation in the fine work of Steven Keeva, Assistant Managing Editor of the *ABA Journal*. Beginning with a series of articles, a number of which are available on his web site (http://www.transformingpractices.com), Keeva explores this idea more systematically in his 1999 book, *Transforming Practices: Finding Joy and Satisfaction in the Legal Life*.[48] Defining "spiritual practices" very broadly, Keeva believes they will "bring out the best in you and help you to know parts of yourself that have been overlooked or pushed aside in response to the demands of a frantic professional life. It will move you toward wholeness, toward accepting yourself for all that you are, so that you can bring your heart and soul to work, find the joy in it, and have more to give to others."[49]

If that sounds appealing, you may want to consider implementing some or all of Keeva's recommended steps "toward balance in your life":

- Spend some time thinking about what parts of yourself you're neglecting. Your body? Your spiritual side? Your need for friendship, love, or intimacy? Your need for connection with your past and your life story?

- Take ten minutes each morning to think about the big picture. Readings from books on spirituality can be helpful.
- Take some time to become aware of your concept of the divine and its place in your life.
- Map out a balanced day, with time allotted for your financial, physical, emotional, and spiritual needs.
- Allow yourself to do nothing for five minutes at least once a day.
- Ask yourself a simple question: How could I spend my days in a way that would make me feel excited about waking up in the morning? The answer may help lead you toward more balance in your life.
- Try this balancing exercise: For the next seven days, keep a diary of your personal and professional time. Notice how much time you devote to each aspect of your life. Then ask yourself if you'd find any adjustments to your time allocation advisable. Are you investing your time in those people, places, and things that you treasure most deeply?
- Don't wait for a huge chunk of free time to materialize before you try these suggestions; find the time where you are now, in the present.[50]

Or, better still, buy the book and absorb dozens of similarly pithy insights.

Like the exhortation to exercise regularly, the value of the other "healthy lifestyle practices" are not the stuff of which controversy is made. They are common sense. Don't work yourself to death. Get a life. Develop hobbies or other serious, nonwork-related interests. Lose yourself in a good book. Keep in touch with your family and friends. Take enough vacation to recharge your batteries. Simple ideas all, but essential if we are to achieve the kind of balanced fulfillment for which many lawyers are properly striving.

And come to think of it, my father was right. You should eat your peas, and go outside—regularly—"to play."

Step 5. Live beneath your means

Points have been made in previous chapters and steps with a common assumption: The individual lawyer has choices to make, and the consequences of those choices can be widely divergent. Will we subscribe to values and priorities—and rigorously apply them—to prevent being swallowed by our work? Will we choose to be a present parent or an available friend over spending another evening or weekend in the office? And, understanding that our profession is more than a dollar-driven business, will we strive not only to become skilled technicians, but also wise counselors, loyal partners, mentors to younger lawyers, or even one of society's "blessed" peacemakers?

The next step is like these previously made points—it implicates priorities and calls on the individual lawyer to make choices—but it may also be more difficult to put into practice. This is particularly true for those who graduate from law school with large educational debts (an irreversible fact). It is also true for those who have made the dubious (but potentially reversible) decision to buy into lifestyles they cannot afford without becoming what Jonathan Foreman calls "wage slaves."[51]

It is doubtful that many who borrow substantial sums to attend college or law school realize how graduating with a large debt can limit choices, but that is precisely what it does. Unlike the decision whether to buy a more prestigious address or a more expensive car, borrowing for educational purposes is often seen as a "necessity." And for some it truly may be.

The fact that borrowing may be (or has been) necessary does not prevent the cycle identified by the ABA's 2000 Pulse Study—the debt-driven need for a high salary leading to unreasonable work demands leading to discontent or worse—from occurring. As the Pulse Study described it, "[y]oung lawyers are often attracted to these positions because the high salaries allow them to more quickly pay off debt owed for law school. . . . Yet these same lawyers, many of whom were the best and the brightest in their respective law school classes, find practicing law [in firms paying the highest salaries] anything but stimulating."[52] In fact, many become positively miserable.

Those who make the unwise, although thoroughly understandable decision to move too quickly from the genteel poverty of the student life into a lifestyle they cannot yet afford are buying a lot more than they realize. They are buying into another cycle, as Stanford Law Professor Deborah L. Rhode put it, in which "desires, once satisfied, beget more desires" and yet "often do not yield enduring satisfactions."[53] And, more pertinent to the matter at hand, they are also—usually without realizing it—dramatically limiting their own options.

In Step 5 we seek to head this cycle off before it begins, and if it has begun, to do whatever we can to reverse it. If you or one of your children are considering how much to borrow for college or law school, do not make the decision lightly. Ask whether attending the much more expensive private school is really worth being saddled with the extra debt *for years* following graduation. It may, in fact, be worth it—the point here is not to make the decision without carefully considering the real-life consequences. And if you are about to graduate from law school, and think a certain starting salary will make your heart's desires immediately affordable, think again!

Living *beneath* your means is the path to financial freedom, the path of maximum options—including the option of telling "Caligula" to go to hell, if necessary—and paradoxically perhaps, even the way to maximize our material pleasures. By controlling our expenses and saving a substantial part of what we make, when we *are* able to afford the nicer car or go on a great vacation (which we will have paid for in advance) —or, for that matter, when we make a generous contribution to a worthy cause—the pleasure will not be compromised by the stress inherent in being overextended financially.

Reflect again on Professor Dershowitz's insight into the irony of friends and former students whose expensive lifestyles lead them to conclude, almost tragically, that they can no longer "afford" to accept what they had long considered "dream jobs."[54] Or the wealthy people who take the shortest vacations because each day away from the office costs them more than the rest of us.[55] This is not what most of us desire when we are thinking clearly, but it will be where many of those who prematurely buy into lifestyles they cannot afford will find themselves somewhere down the road. Professor Dershowitz hits this nail right on the head when he warns that "[w]hen money enslaves rather than liberates, something is wrong."[56]

Johnny Cash grew up poor and became a highly paid entertainer. But he never forgot how it felt to be poor or lost the common touch. I recall reading years ago that Johnny Cash always carried thousands of dollars in his wallet. Having lived without, he enjoyed the freedom inherent in having extra money on hand. Although his means were higher than most of ours, he had discovered the value of spending less than he made.

Realistically, even absent large educational debts or the manic pursuit of material acquisitions, as the repairman once told the author, "life ain't cheap." Just as work expands to fill the time, so our financial "needs" have a tendency to expand and consume all we make—and sometimes a good portion of what we hope to make in the future. Cars now cost more than houses did when the author graduated from law school (in 1976), for goodness sake. The upshot is that, unless we actively struggle against it, we will find ourselves engaging in consumer spending that severely limits our ability to choose a healthier, more balanced life. How, after all, can we say "No" to more fee-generating work when we have all those bills to pay?

But if we are to live a balanced life we must learn to say "No" not only to more work, but also to the consumer spending that seems to make imbalance a necessity. By controlling our spending, we can significantly reduce the financial pressures that stress us out and push an increasing number over the edge. We can take "Step 5" toward fulfillment in the contemporary practice of law. We can live beneath our means.

Step 6. Don't let technology control your life

Some years ago a speaker held forth on how three technological innovations, also known as "modern conveniences," had actually robbed us of a great deal of our free time. The three culprits were the telephone, air-conditioning, and the photocopy machine.

It was one of those talks that made you smile and think, "I never thought of it that way." Although it is a good bet that few, if any, in the audience used these conveniences less following the presentation, it certainly made you think. Unlike more predictable personal visits, the telephone had rendered us "on call" at almost any time (although I do remember being taught as a child never to call anyone at home after 9:00 P.M., and as a young lawyer not to call anyone at the office before 9:00 A.M.). Air-conditioning, especially in the South, extended our nine-to-ten-month work year—court would shut down, and many lawyers would go to the beach, lake, or mountains during the hottest part of the summer—to twelve. And the transition from carbon paper to copier greatly expanded our concept of who "needs to know" about various documents, with all that entails. One does not have to be a Luddite[57] to get the point: technology is, as the ABA Pulse Study described it in 2000, a "double-edged sword."[58]

Of course, the technological innovations have continued unabated. As will be the case with some readers, our children were more adept with the computer before they got out of grade school than we parents will probably ever be. But even for us relative Neanderthals, the computer is an omnipresent part of our daily lives. Virtually all lawyers (and judges and law professors) now do legal research online or on a CD, not with books or in a library. E-mail is the preferred way to communicate with many clients and lawyers, and indeed, some clients require it. The Internet is a must-use resource from the various research sites to information on expert witnesses to the ability to retrieve or file documents. Even as you are reading this chapter, to paraphrase what Bob Dylan sang to us boomers, The technology it is still a-changin'.

So what is wrong with all that? Nothing, really; and even if there were some preferable features of the earlier approach—having days instead of minutes to respond to communications, for example—we will never put the technological genie back in the bottle. Time and technology will continue to move rapidly along, with or without us, as it did after Ned Ludd and those named for him took to destroying "labor-saving" machinery in eighteenth and nineteenth century England.[59]

We can, however, note the additional pressure proximately caused by technology, and seek to humanize it a bit. And we can take Step 6, that is, we can refuse to let technology invade and control every inch of our lives.

Here is how the ABA Pulse Study described pressures caused by the "growing dependence on technology":

- Lawyers feel compelled to stay up on technology, yet they don't know where to turn.
- Lawyers are also finding it increasingly difficult to mentally disengage or escape from work when at home or on vacation.
- Less-personalized communication both diminishes lawyers' ability to develop relationships with clients and can lead to miscommunication.
- Work itself has become more rushed and less considered.
- Instantaneous access to information pushes performance standards higher:
  - Clients expect fast turnaround on research and the remittance of documents.
  - Courts and clients expect legal work to reflect the most up-to-date decisions posted on the Internet.[60]

The Pulse Study also noted the negative impact technology-related pressures were having on professional satisfaction:

- Practicing law is less personal and more mechanized.
- Younger lawyers often spend the bulk of their time in front of a computer screen, which is less stimulating and intrinsically satisfying.
- Lawyers find it increasingly difficult to put their stamp of professionalism on their work.[61]

Or, as one lawyer in a focus group—categorized as a "Firm Decisionmaker" in Sacramento, California—put it, the problem is *too much* information. This lawyer reports, for example, receiving about 150 e-mails a day, on which he must spend up to "an hour every day just going through them. That type of information is an information glut. . . . I don't seem to ever get away from it."[62]

Think about it. If this lawyer left his computer at the office and took a two-week vacation, as he or she certainly should from time to time, upon returning to the office there would be over 3,000 e-mails, which would take about a day and a half simply to scroll through and read. Is it technologically backwards to say this is "just nuts?"

The Pulse Study also elaborated on the effect the many hours spent glued to the computer is having on professional satisfaction. Not surprisingly, the news is not good:

> Except for lawyers who are involved in trial work, most lawyers spend the bulk of their first years sitting, day after day, in front of a computer terminal conducting somewhat tedious tasks—creating/filling out forms, researching issues, reviewing documents, etc. There is little opportunity to interact with—and thus learn from—other lawyers. Because these mundane tasks are the very source of billable hours, young lawyers also feel guilty about spending any time away from their desks. And, in law firms where new lawyers are paid high salaries, how much time one spends away from the computer "not working" is carefully scrutinized.[63]

This lack of collegiality, not to mention human contact with actual clients, catches many newly admitted lawyers by surprise. "One thing . . . I was not prepared for," one "New Bar Admittee" in Chicago told an ABA focus group, was "sitting in your office by yourself, alone, all day long, with a max of five minutes of human contact. I didn't think it would be like that. I wasn't prepared mentally and emotionally for that."[64]

Nor is the daily dose of technology necessarily over when it is finally time to go home. There is always the home computer, or a laptop or notebook computer, to be taken home to "finish up." Many lawyers are expected to go nowhere without a cell phone, beeper, or both, in case someone needs to reach them. Many are expected to check voice mail and e-mail regularly, even if further work has to wait until "first thing in the morning." (Dare you be so lax?)

Again, the Pulse Study—rightly calling technology "both a blessing and a curse"—draws an accurate picture of the dilemma faced by the contemporary lawyer who hopes to excel professionally, but also wants to have "a life":

> On the one hand, laptops, beepers, cell phones and other technological gadgetry allow these responsibility-laden lawyers to take work home with them so they won't miss their daughter's soccer game or their son's Boy Scout meeting. Technology also allows them to operate more efficiently which, at least in theory, frees up time they can spend with their families or on personal pursuits. The downside, of course, is that these very advancements have blurred the lines between office and home. Now it is impossible to escape the demands of the office. Many lawyers feel enslaved to check voice mail and e-mail regularly. Even those who have established boundaries realize these tenets may or may not be respected by clients or colleagues.[65]

Technology *is* both a blessing and a curse. Some clients and partners expect to be given home phone numbers, cell phone numbers, and beeper numbers—and proceed to use them liberally. Expectations that associates and even partners will be in regular touch with the office electronically, wherever they are and whatever they are doing, are clearly communicated. Can any professional advancement, any interim material acquisition, really be worth this kind of omnipresent invasion of our privacy and personal space?

The answer, class, is "Of course not!" (Or, if you wish, stronger language to that effect.)

So how do we counter the technology-driven pressure to be, in effect, on duty or on call "24/7"? Although it is no easy project, and to the extent we are attempting to roll back our current over-availability it may be even more difficult, it starts with drawing a line. As in the decision about how many hours to spend at the office generally, we must each decide how much of us is "for sale." And then if our clients, employers, or partners do not like it, tough luck.

Once we get up the courage to draw the line—and it will take courage—two basic things can happen. Those who have been applying this kind of pervasive pressure might realize we can perform adequately without being at their beck and call 100 percent of the time. In that event we will have successfully adjusted their unreasonable expectations and gotten back that part of our personal lives we never should have given up. The other thing that can happen, of course, is that we might lose clients or even lose our jobs. Although this would no doubt be a temporary hardship, things will eventually fall into place—and be far better, overall, when they do. Remember, we are not advocating being lazy or shirking duty here. We are talking about working long and hard, but at some point realizing that we share every human being's need for private space.

How we do that precisely is something each individual must work out. Some get up early and work, either at home or in their offices, so they can have dinner with their families most evenings. Others decline to carry cell phones or beepers, or check e-mail or voice mail, much of the time they are away from the office. The author knows a family that takes the phone off the hook for a brief time in the evenings to allow the family some uninterrupted time together. But whatever our particular strategy, the core objective is the same: to establish boundaries that prevent technology from controlling our lives, taking Step 6 toward fulfillment in the contemporary practice of law.

Step 7. Care about character—and conduct yourself accordingly

"Let me tell you how you will start acting unethically," Professor Schiltz addresses law students. "It will begin with your time sheets."[66] Schiltz's prediction of what might follow is eerily prescient:

> One day, not too long after you start practicing law, you will sit down at the end of a long, tiring day, and you just won't have much to show for your efforts in terms of billable hours. It will be near the end of the month. You will know that all of the partners will be looking at your monthly time report in a few days, so what you'll do is pad your time sheet just a bit. Maybe you will bill a client for 90 minutes for a task that really took you only 60 minutes to perform. However, you will promise yourself that you will repay the client at the first opportunity by doing

> thirty minutes of work for the client for "free." In this way, you will be "borrowing," not "stealing."
>
> And then what will happen is that it will become easier and easier to take these little loans against future work. And then, after a while, you will stop paying back these little loans. You will convince yourself that, although you billed for 90 minutes and spent only 60 minutes on the project, you did such good work that your client should pay a bit more for it. After all, your billing rate is awfully low, and your client is awfully rich.
>
> And then you will pad more and more—every two-minute telephone conversation will go down on the sheet as ten minutes, every three-hour research project will go down with an extra quarter hour or so. You will continue to rationalize your dishonesty to yourself in various ways until one day you stop doing even that. And, before long—it won't take you much more than three or four years—you will be stealing from your clients almost every day, and you won't even notice it.[67]

Or, to put it in philosophical jargon, once we start down the slippery slope of ethical compromise—lying, cheating, or stealing just a little, perhaps—it is awfully difficult to prevent a full slide into shameless dishonesty.

If our aim is fulfillment in the practice of law, or in life generally, we must not let that happen. If we steal from our clients, a little or a lot, it will become increasingly difficult to feel good about who we are and what we do for a living, to "look ourselves in the mirror," or to sleep well at night. We will become more cynical about the whole idea of right and wrong, condemning at least in our minds "moral absolutists" who might take issue with our real-world pragmatism. And an overall sense of fulfillment, difficult to achieve at best, will become more elusive still.

Professor Schiltz also warns the law student looking ahead at his or her career about "becom[ing] a liar."[68] Here is his similar take on the contours of that slippery slope:

> A deadline will come up one day, and, for reasons that are not entirely your fault, you will not be able to meet it. So you will call your senior partner or your client and make up a white lie for why you missed the deadline. And then you will get busy and a partner will ask whether you proofread a lengthy prospectus and you will say yes, even though you didn't. And then you will be drafting a brief and you will quote language from a Supreme Court opinion even though you will know that, when

> read in context, the language does not remotely suggest what you are implying it suggests. And then, in preparing a client for a deposition, you will help the client to formulate an answer to a difficult question that will likely be asked—an answer that will be "legally accurate" but that will mislead your opponent. And then you will be reading through a big box of your client's documents—a box that has not been opened in twenty years—and you will find a document that would hurt your client's case, but that no one except you knows exists, and you will simply "forget" to produce it in response to your opponent's discovery requests.[69]

"Do you see what will happen?" the professor rhetorically intones. "After a couple of years of this, you won't even notice that you are lying and cheating and stealing every day that you practice law."[70] A little padding of the time sheet here, a half-truth or "little white lie to cover a missed deadline there" will have fundamentally changed "your entire frame of [moral] reference."[71] Sadly, lawyers who slide all the way into this amoral abyss will have adopted "a set of values that embodies not what is right or wrong, but what is profitable, what [they] can get away with."[72]

Do not let it happen to you, and if compromised ethics have already infected "the hundreds of mundane things that [we lawyers] do almost unthinkingly every day,"[73] vow and strive to return to a more solid ethical and moral foundation. However much pressure is being applied, "[d]o not pad your time sheets—even once. And do not tell lies to partners or clients or opposing counsel. And do not misrepresent legal authority to judges. And do not break your promises. And do not do anything else that is contrary to the values you now hold."[74] Or, if you have already gone a way down the slippery slope and reform is necessary, return and "hold on for dear life" to the values you were taught and never should have compromised.

Of course, there is more to having good character than not lying, cheating, or stealing. Presumably a lawyer with good character, whether or not a religious person, will apply what has come to be known as the Golden Rule ("Do unto others as you would have them do unto you"—not the cynic's version, "*before* they do unto you.").

If more lawyers would accept and apply this simple precept—treating others as they would wish to be treated—many of the ills inherent in contemporary practice would be addressed ipso facto. Certainly, the return to collegiality and civility, a core concern of the professionalism movement, would be. Ditto for the prompt return of phone calls and response to correspondence, full cooperation during discovery, and the general need to reduce aggression and stress, which is over the top for altogether too many practitioners.

The ABA Pulse Study noted as "Pressure Point #6" what it called "an erosion of professional courtesy and sense of community" in the contemporary practice.[75] Professor Roger E. Schechter called it "the civility crises" in his 1997 article, "Changing Law Schools to Make Less Nasty Lawyers."[76] Professor Schechter describes the perceived problem as lawyers who are "increasingly prone to behave as combatants, refusing to extend common courtesies to one another. Sometimes called the 'Rambo' style of litigation, it includes such practices as refusing to return phone calls, grant routine extensions of deadlines, or even shake hands in court, along with more abrasive and hostile behaviors such as vulgarity and name-calling, shouting, temper tantrums, or even occasional fisticuffs during depositions."[77]

Not the kind of behavior, in a word, one would expect from a lawyer of good character, and certainly not from a lawyer who is striving to practice in accordance with the Golden Rule. And yet it is behavior that is sufficiently pervasive that in one survey "half the lawyers responding characterized their professional colleagues as 'obnoxious,'"[78] and for a trial judge to report that "a persistent complaint of jurors concerns the unpleasant atmosphere of the courtroom, caused by lawyers snarling at each other, making absurd objections, and badgering witnesses."[79]

The ABA's Pulse Study notes less-dramatic lapses in civility, but points to essentially the same phenomenon. Noting the "erosion of . . . common courtesy," which has led to a "less pleasant and more stressed work environment" for many lawyers, the 2000 report explains:

- In the past, lawyers from various professional backgrounds would get together in more relaxed settings—bar meetings, the lawyer's room at the courthouse, etc.—where they could get to know one another on a more personal basis. It was in this setting that codes of behavior were established and conveyed to younger lawyers.
- While a sense of community still exists, it now occurs at a specialty level.
- Lawyers today think of themselves as "trial lawyers," "patent specialists," or "defense lawyers," beholden only to the rules of their specific community.

- Younger lawyers, who have never been taught by mentors or the community at large about the professional codes of behavior, may confuse advocacy with aggression.[80]

The result of this "erosion in professional courtesy" is more than just the absence of the camaraderie enjoyed in years past. It has also given rise to a pervasive distrust *by lawyers* of other lawyers. As a Birmingham, Alabama lawyer told one of the ABA focus groups, for example, "I've gotten to the point where I almost can't trust anybody on the other side of the case."[81] Or, as a California lawyer more bluntly put it in another focus group, some lawyers now confuse "advocacy" with "asshole."[82]

Of course, some rough-and-tumble is to be expected in the relations of those who essentially argue and fight for a living. And as we have seen in an earlier chapter, lawyer conduct in prior generations was far from perfect. Professor Glendon relates, for example, an exchange one of her colleagues overheard in a Chicago courtroom in the early 1960s between a judge and a lawyer suspected of being under the influence:

"Counsel, the court believes it smells alcohol on counsel's breath."

"Is that so, Your Honor?" came the quick reply. "Well, counsel believes he smells garlic on the court's breath."[83]

But conceding imperfections of the past, can contemporary lawyers do better on the character/professional relations front? Of course we can—much better, in fact. We can vow to do what most of us already know is right: We can strive to conduct ourselves honorably, which means refusing to lie, cheat, or steal—however much pressure we are under, or however "profitable" the wrong choice may appear to be at that moment.

We can adopt the simple but profound teaching of the Golden Rule: that we should treat others, including opposing counsel, as we ourselves would like to be treated. If we do that—refusing to start down the slippery slope of compromised ethics, and treating others with civility and respect—we will like what we see when we look in the mirror. If we care about our character and conduct ourselves accordingly, we will be able to sleep well at night. And we will have taken one more important step toward finding satisfaction and fulfillment in the practice of law.

Step 8. "Just say no" to some clients

It is difficult to say whether changes in lawyering, including the dishonest billing practices (by some) described by Professor Schiltz,[84] preceded the more recently noted changes in clients, but there is no doubt lawyer-client relations have changed significantly. Like those in lawyering generally, the changes in clients and client relations generally have not been for the better.

The parallel changes in lawyering and clients make it difficult to discuss one without continual reference to the other, almost like hearing "both sides" following an argument between two children. "OK, you did this, and you did that. I don't care if A or B. From now on X, Y, and Z." In other words, before stones are thrown at the unreasonable or unethical demands of some clients, lawyers must be sure their own glass houses are in order.

Traditional exhortations to lawyers, like those of Ambassador Linowitz "not [to] undertake the representation of someone he does not trust and whose story he does not believe,"[85] almost strike the contemporary ear as naive and quaint. But Ambassador Linowitz is onto something that is still relevant to the topic at hand. There remains a kernel of truth in the conclusion of Roy Grutman, a senior partner in a New York megafirm, that "accepting a client is ultimately a moral decision."[86]

According to this traditional view, "[p]rofessionalism requires a lawyer to tell any client that he will not introduce evidence he believes to be false or seek to discredit by trickery testimony he believes to be true, and if the client wants other services, the lawyer should urge him to seek representation from a lawyer who considers him truthful."[87] (I can almost hear Professor Dershowitz tearing apart this appealing, if somewhat absolutist, statement in a Socratic dialogue.) Contrast this more traditional, morally based approach to client selection, to the description of the "ideal client" by Walt Bachman's former partner as a "wholly unreasonable rich man."[88] Bachman's partner simply followed the assumption that law is a dollar-driven business to its logical conclusion, reasoning that the client's "unreasonableness creates the demand for lawyers, and he must be rich to pay their fees."[89]

Pleading for a return to value-based client selection, Ambassador Linowitz urges that "[g]ood lawyers don't have to take bad clients."[90] He relates a conversation with Edward Bennett Williams in which the famous trial lawyer was asked about his representation of certain sordid characters. "Everyone is entitled to a lawyer," Williams defended himself (with some justification). "Yes," came the more traditional response, "but they are not entitled to *you*."[91]

Fast-forwarding two or three decades, Linowitz points to the savings-and-loan scandal as being "laced with stories about the participation of reputable law firms that knew their clients were doing improper things but tried to squeeze their actions into the framework of permissive government regulations so they could be, with luck, legally defensible."[92] Exercising 20-20 hindsight, he notes that regulators subsequently decided both "that the dishonesty [of the savings-and-loan employees] was punishable" and "that the lawyers bear some responsibility for abetting it."[93] When the president denounces trial lawyers in his State of the Union message, for which he received a bipartisan standing ovation, one has to wonder how long aggressive prosecutors will give lawyers the traditional benefit of the doubt in deciding whom to charge as a "co-conspirator" in more politically driven initiatives.

Again, Ambassador Linowitz expresses the traditional view, which will not comfort lawyers tempted to walk close to the frequently fuzzy line between zealous advocacy and abetting a fraud:

> [I]n the end professionals have to stand responsible for their own actions, and the cry "My client made me do it" must fall on deaf ears. Harris Weinstein, who as general counsel for the Office of Thrift Supervision brought most of the cases against the law firms that represented the S&Ls, found himself "hard pressed . . . to understand how we can claim that a lawyer is free to deceive a third party when the client could not. If that were the rule, if a lawyer were permitted to do that, what would be left of the liability risked by the client's deception? Any client could overcome that liability simply by hiring a lawyer to do the dirty work for him."[94]

This is not to suggest that lawyers should shy away from politically unpopular causes or clients, or even be less zealous in their advocacy, but fundamental self-interest requires some very clear ethical thinking as we step closer to this line. Lawyers who fail to maintain high ethical standards and appropriate professional distance from what a politically motivated prosecutor might regard as "deception" could find *themselves* in need of counsel. Right or wrong, that is particularly true in today's antilawyer political environment.

While most lawyers will not get close enough to this line to have a reasonable fear of criminal prosecution, many more describe the lawyer-client relationship as increasingly stressful and problematic.

Walt Bachman summarily calls it "the most stressful aspect of lawyering."[95] The ABA Pulse Study concluded that "increasingly demanding clients" was "Pressure Point #2" in contemporary practice.[96] And according to Steven Keeva, assistant managing editor of the *ABA Journal*, a certain number of lawyers have realized this and are now choosing their clients more carefully.[97]

The ABA Pulse Study describes how increased client influence over "how legal projects are priced and executed" has become a major "pressure point":

- Clients tend to be project, not relationship-focused.
- Projects are often bid out to multiple firms rather than turning to one trusted counselor.
- There is an increasing desire for project fees, which can be budgeted, versus billable hours, with law firms assuming the risk if projects require more effort than anticipated.
- Clients also demand fast turnaround and 24/7 access to lawyers, at least via e-mail.
- Many want to be directly involved in the process.
- Billing is carefully scrutinized.
- Larger clients may require firms to follow formal billing procedures specific to their organization's requirements.
- Lack of uniformity in billing procedures means firms often have to utilize multiple billing approaches.[98]

Whether "increasingly demanding clients" were caused in whole or in part by increasingly greedy, dishonest lawyers is beside the point here. The impact on professional satisfaction, like the proverbial rain in the *Bible*, has fallen "on the just and the unjust."[99] According to the Pulse Study, this means:

- More time/resources spent on administrative tasks and relationship management
- Less control over the pace of work
- Less ability to escape the pressures of the job
- Ambiguity as to what and how to bill
- Lower profits/job, requiring lawyers to take on more work
- Feeling more like a "hired gun" versus a respected counselor[100]

Or, as a California lawyer told one of the ABA focus groups, "It strikes me that the clients are shopping on eBay for their next lawyer."[101]

Steven Keeva introduces us to two New York litigators who ultimately decided it was in their best interest, as they tell schoolkids in regard to alcohol and drugs, to "just say no" to some clients. Sheldon ("Shelly") Tashman, who once took any case that walked through the door, has since become a personal injuries lawyer who "will not take a case he doesn't believe in."[102]

"The law has many temptations that lack integrity," Tashman concluded. "There's a temptation to make a case out of nothing, to make a living out of situations that aren't real, to not be ethical."[103] Admitting "certain things [that] weren't really right" in his past, he cites "trouble sleeping" and the specter of his son seeing an unfavorable newspaper story as the dual motivation for changes in his professional course.[104] Tashman quickly discovered that the peace of mind attending higher ethics and more careful client selection were well worth what they cost him in lost fees.

Stephen Chakwin, who met Tashman when they were on opposite sides of a case, was sufficiently inspired by Tashman's good example that he decided to make significant changes in his own practice. Sharing the desire for work in which he really believed, Chakwin gave up his partnership in a medium-sized New York firm. He now practices with one other lawyer and spends a portion of his time "coaching unhappy lawyers toward finding a more satisfying path."[105]

Perhaps the most colorful approach to client relations was taken by Walt Bachman in *Law v. Life: What Lawyers Are Afraid to Say About the Legal Profession*. In a chapter titled "The APC Factor: The Truth About Clients," Bachman recollects how he came out of law school hoping for "sweet ladies like Ms. Palsgraf" (of the famous *Palsgraf* case fame) as clients.[106] It did not take him long to realize, however, that "very few billable hours are racked up in pursuit of vindication for such totally faultless clients."[107]

Instead of finding himself representing the rare Ms. Palgrafs of the client world, Walt Bachman discovered that "in many cases neither side is pleasant to represent" and, in fact, that in a significant percentage of cases, his firm's clients were "assholes."[108]

Which brings us back to the chapter title. The APC Factor, as it turns out, stands for "Assholes Per Capita."[109] Engaging in highly sophisticated social science, Bachman (no doubt utilizing intellectual and academic skills sharpened during his years at Oxford on a Rhodes Scholarship) proposes a formula. Stated generally, the formula to determine the APC Factor in a given situation is:

$$\frac{\text{Assholes}}{\text{Total Population}} = \text{The APC Factor}$$[110]

Tongue now firmly in cheek, Bachman proceeds to apply what we might call AA (Asshole Analysis), to the world of law. In the instance of American litigation clients, this formula would be more specifically stated as:

$$\frac{\text{Asshole Litigation Clients}}{\text{Total Litigation Clients}} = \text{Litigation-Client APC Factor}$$

For example, if we take the total number of new litigation clients in America last year (say, 2,000,000) and determine the number of those litigants independently and objectively determined to be assholes (say approximately 800,000), the APC Factor is derived as follows:

$$\frac{\text{800,000 Asshole Clients}}{\text{2,000,000 Total Clients}} = .40 \text{ APC Factor}$$[111]

Conceding the need for further research, Bachman draws on his own experience and that of his lawyer friends to suggest an APC Factor for litigation clients "in the vicinity of .4 and rising."[112] Estimating the APC Factor for society at large as "closer to .1," Bachman reaches the compelling conclusion that "the APC Factor for [litigation] clients is four times that of the overall populace."[113] Of course, it remains with each individual lawyer to decide how this seminal research should be applied to his or her practice!

On a bit more serious note, to increase satisfaction in lawyer-client relations, Steven Keeva suggests a broader and deeper look at the client's motivation, expectations, and best interest (broadly defined). Among other questions, Keeva suggests that lawyers consider at the outset:

Why has the client come? Is he/she driven by

- anger?
- a sense of having been victimized?
- a desire to heal?

What role does he want me to take?

Am I seeing the whole person, or focusing narrowly on the possible legal issues?

Are my words consistent with my values?

Have I made clear what I see both his/her and my own role(s) to be in this relationship?

Have I made clear where my loyalties lie—to him/her, yes, but perhaps also to minimizing conflict, to the other side, or to the community?

Have I been clear about the range of options, both legal and nonlegal, that may be available?[114]

As the representation continues, Keeva encourages lawyers who hope for improved relationships with their clients to ask, *inter alia*:

Have I been clear so far about what I see as the merits and deficiencies in the case the client thinks he/she has?

Does the client seem open to striving for a win/win solution?

- What might such a solution look like in this case? (Even better, ask the client this.)

Is the client willing to take any responsibility for the problem? If he/she is willing to forgo the role of victim, what opportunities does that open up?

- Can the client admit that there were things he/she could have done that might have prevented the current problem? If so, can the client take an active role in resolving it?

Does the client appear to need permission to let go of his/her anger, and would the client accept that permission from me?

Is the client deluding him/herself about any aspect of the case?

What ways of looking at this case might locate deeper meanings and broader implications? For example, are there family implications that may at first not be apparent?

Community issues? Spiritual issues for the client? How might these implications matter?[115]

While some will understandably balk at these wide-ranging questions, others will be pleasantly surprised at how much certain clients appreciate having a lawyer who can think outside the technical box. This is not to suggest, of course, that the lawyer become a scold, telling every client how to get back on the straight and narrow path. Rather, these questions are intended to help *the client* decide what "best interest" might mean in a particular case.

To summarize the ground covered under what we are calling "Step 8," we have seen that there is more stress than there once was in lawyer-client relations. Part of this is the fault of lawyers, particularly greedy, dishonest lawyers. But wherever relative fault lies, we can increase the inherent satisfaction in the lawyer-client relationship by keeping in mind a few key principles.

First, we must be scrupulously honest with our clients, including but not limited to the work we choose to do and how it is billed. Second, we need to be exceedingly careful not to cross ethical lines and to keep a measure of professional distance, particularly where an objective third party might see our client's conduct as "deceptive." Third, we should strive to provide wise counsel, which often requires more of a "big-picture" approach to problem solving and conflict resolution. And finally, perhaps applying Brother Bachman's brilliant AA, we will simply have to "just say no" to some clients.

Step 9. Stay emotionally healthy

How we spend the hours of our lives is not the only balance we must strike. Finding balance between the rational/cognitive/left-brain elements of human experience—where many lawyers are at their best—and the "softer" right-brain counterbalances, including feelings, emotion, "heart," and imagination, is just as important. In a word, it is crucial that we stay emotionally healthy.

Lawyers who achieve professional success, but who are *not* emotionally balanced and healthy, will frequently realize that "something is missing." Some seek professional help, particularly if the result is clinical depression, a failed marriage, or some other personal crisis. Others may muddle along in what Benjamin Sells calls a "state of mild torpor"[116] for years.

As Dr. Sells analyzes the problem, by prolonged overemphasis on the rational and the argumentative, many "lawyers have become abstracted from the world of actual experience. . . . Whether in terms of feeling like a fungible component in a big law firm machine, or a sideline spectator of one's own family life, or like an amoral technician servicing the bottom line . . . lawyers feel dissociated from daily life—*including themselves*."[117] At its worst, this can leave even highly successful lawyers feeling "lonely . . . exiled, rejected by their fellow citizens."[118]

But whether or not it devolves to that point, many lawyers need "[t]o reestablish contact with the ground of actual experience, [to] break through the abstractions that separate them from air below the clouds. They must come back to earth, where the air is thicker and more life-sustaining."[119] According to Sells, "this means that lawyers need to educate their passions and invigorate their imaginations with the same dedication they apply to sharpening their analytic skills."[120]

As Professor Walter Bennett sees it, the goal is no less than "wholeness as a human being," which may require "a reorientation of the soul . . . , a reopening of the intellectual and emotional gates that so many people begin to shut in law school."[121] George W. Kaufman, whose workshops for unhappy or stressed-out lawyers were noted in chapter 2,[122] would agree. Noting the importance of "intimacy" to happiness, and the need to be in touch with feelings and emotions to achieve it, Kaufman traces the imbalance he has observed in many lawyers back to his years at Yale Law School—from 1959 to 1962! "Only once in my three years at law school," he writes, "did I witness a professor blush because he had revealed a deeply personal side of himself, and I never observed any teachers or students express feelings with the same fervor they expounded facts."[123]

As it turns out, a hyper-rationalist approach to education and life distorts more than the individual personality. It also limits our ability to grasp the real meaning of many human experiences. "Feelings and emotions are part of our human makeup [that] give us information in a way that is different from the way we gather information through our intellect," Kaufman notes.[124] Imbalance occurs in the lives and personalities of many lawyers, beginning in law school, because "[o]ur training honors our cognitive skills and dismisses information gathered through other channels. As such, we tend to exploit our rational capacities and ignore other parts of ourselves that offer different ways of learning."[125]

In an article titled "A Symphony of Silence,"[126] Steven Keeva likens lawyers with undeveloped or atrophied inner lives to music that is off-key and lacking rhythm. "Nearly all that is audible," he concludes, (comparing the profession at large to a symphony orchestra) "is shrill, frenetic, and in the upper registers. The bass line seems to be missing. . . . There's something wrong with the rhythm, too. There are too few rests. Music without silence grows tedious and exhausting; it gives the imagination no room to breathe."[127]

Keeva's prescription for lawyers who have focused excessively "on striving and achieving," who find themselves mired in "tedious and exhausting" pursuit of "airtight, left-brain solutions at the expense of feeling and intuition," is what he broadly calls "inner work."[128] Acknowledging that ours is "a culture that rewards workaholism and downplays the value of stillness and reflection," Keeva urges lawyers who hope for happiness to reconnect with these kinder, gentler elements of the human experience.[129]

In *The Lawyer's Guide to Balancing Life and Work: Taking the Stress Out of Success,* George Kaufman recognizes that some lawyers feel "happy" when levels of professional success, such as making partner, are reached. For these, "there has been a joining of success and happiness. For others, the gulf between success and happiness is deep."[130] Kaufman's response, like Steven Keeva's exhortation to engage in "inner work," is not rocket science. "When I began my career," Kaufman writes, "I assumed that success would yield happiness. It doesn't. If happiness is to be a career goal, it must be separately addressed."[131]

In his 35 years in practice, George Kaufman certainly knew lawyers who "owned" their values and had well-integrated personalities, that is, lawyers who were emotionally healthy. But he also encountered those who were professionally successful, yet "enjoy[ed] no sense of well-being," who felt "trapped by the work they [did]," and many others whose "work life ha[d] invaded their privacy."[132] He writes, for example, about a lawyer acquaintance "who, when admitted to partnership in a prestigious law firm, was overwhelmed with sadness and dread. Eight years of toil had produced membership in an exclusive club. But the work he endured to achieve that membership was work he would need to endure forever to keep that membership in good standing."[133]

In his writing and in the seminars he conducts, Kaufman promotes emotional health through a series of simple exercises. In one, he invites participants to consider the opportunity costs (which he calls "losses") of a demanding professional life. "Those losses started with compromises we made as we attempted to juggle work, play, family, and self. If the term 'loss' seems too stark to describe your process, consider what you may have compromised or surrendered to succeed at work."[134]

Kaufman makes an interesting observation about a preliminary hurdle in getting lawyers to describe their feelings. "Losses are connected to our feelings," he explains. "But when I ask lawyers to describe those feelings, most deny their existence. In fact, whenever I ask lawyers to tell me their feelings, they respond by telling me their thoughts."[135] But although they may be deeply buried, getting back in touch with feelings about these "losses" or opportunity costs—from harm to an intimate relationship, to an inability to pursue a hobby or do volunteer work, to missing a child's birthday—is a necessary ingredient of emotional health.

In another exercise, Kaufman encourages lawyers to reflect on their ten most-important values. To set the reflection in motion—and, hopefully, to engage the right-brain imagination—Kaufman offers a nonexclusive list of values we may want to consider:[136]

Love	Freedom	Security	Play
Power	Comfort	Competence	Exercise
Growth	Joy	Creativity	Vegging Out
Acceptance	Support	Warmth	Pride
Gratefulness	Honesty	Balance	Romance
Justice	Serenity	Humility	Frivolity
Trust	Fulfillment	Success	Spontaneity
Intimacy	Adventure	Passion	Perfection
Health	Service	Achievement	Appreciation
Humor	Harmony	Winning	Conscientiousness
Focus	Kindness	Appreciation	Wealth
Integrity	Desire	Presence	Aggressiveness
Honor	Family	Change	Tenacity
Beauty	Truthfulness	Understanding	Practicality
Expediency	Inquiry	Compassion	Loyalty

Of course, while some values are certainly more commendable than others, the purpose of this exercise is not to tell us what our values should be. Rather, the purpose here is to cause us to reflect on what our foundational values *are*—and then to be honest with ourselves about whether and how well we are putting them into practice.

However clear our "values" or pure our priorities, the high stress level at which many lawyers operate week after week will make emotional health and balance difficult to achieve. Fortunately, there is help available here, too, but as in the related issues we have already addressed—like establishing clear priorities, developing and practicing good time management, implementing healthy lifestyle practices, living beneath our means, not letting technology control our lives, and just saying "no" to some clients—the stress problem will not resolve on its own. Like the other issues, reducing excessive stress is an ongoing struggle in which we must actively engage.

The late Peter N. Kutulakis, Professor of Law and Vice Dean at the Dickenson School of Law in Carlisle, Pennsylvania, became one of a growing number of experts in "stress management" specifically for lawyers. In his contribution to the ABA's 1997 book, *Living with the Law: Strategies to Avoid Burnout and Create Balance*, Professor Kutulakis (who holds law and counseling degrees) suggests that we think of four key areas in which lawyers need to practice effective stress management: (1) Managing Your Body; (2) Managing Your Personal and Emotional Life: (3) Managing Relations With Your Clients; and (4) Managing Relations With Your Coworkers.[137] As in Dr. Amiram Elwork's helpful book, *Stress Management for Lawyers: How to Increase Personal and Professional Satisfaction in the Law,*[138] Kutulakis's recommendations range from reorienting fundamental priorities and values to simple but effective relaxation techniques.

To reduce stress, Professor Kutulakis recommended several strategies that by now should be familiar: balancing work and personal life, regular exercise, saying "no" to the demands of some clients, and effective time management.[139] But both he and Dr. Elwork bring their treatment/therapy training to the conversation, also recommending conscious relaxation, deep breathing, visualization, biofeedback, and what Kutulakis calls "thought stopping."[140] Lawyers suffering from high stress should consider these recommendations, as well as the very similar "Stress-Reducing Suggestions" in George Kaufman's materials.[141]

Whether we use Kaufman's, Kutulakis's, or Elwork's exercises, follow Keeva's advice concerning "inner work," or take alternative routes, if we are to find fulfillment in law or life, we must take Step 9. We must seek a healthy balance between our rational, cognitive sides, on the one hand, and our feelings, emotions, hearts, and imaginations on the other. We must pursue balance not only in how we spend the limited hours of our lives but also between our outer and inner selves. In a word, we must strive to stay emotionally healthy.

Step 10. Embrace law as a "high calling"

As we saw in chapter 1, even those who agree with Yale Law School Dean Anthony Kronman that the legal profession is "in danger of losing its soul"[142] presume that it once had one. Indeed, the very title of Dean Kronman's provocative 1993 book, *The Lost Lawyer: Failing Ideals of the Legal Profession,* implies that the profession was once *not* lost, that its failing ideals were once healthy and widely held.

This is certainly Dean Kronman's view. "The [spiritual] crisis has been brought about," he writes, "by the demise of an older set of values that until quite recently played a vital role in defining the aspirations of American lawyers."[143] And at the heart of this "older set of values" was an *assumption* that the best lawyer was "not simply an accomplished technician but a person of prudence or practical wisdom as well . . . a wisdom about human beings and their tangled affairs that anyone who wishes to provide real deliberative counsel must possess."[144]

It is not our purpose here to rehash this historical or philosophical point, but to suggest its connection with professional satisfaction and fulfillment—a connection Dean Kronman also clearly sees. "To those who shared this view it seemed obvious that a lawyer's life could be deeply fulfilling. For the character-virtue of practical wisdom is a central human excellence that has an intrinsic value of its own. So long as the cultivation of this virtue remained an important professional ideal, lawyers could therefore be confident that their work had intrinsic value, too."[145]

Lovely old words: wisdom, virtue, character. Hardly ones that come immediately to mind when the contemporary lawyer is considered, but words or ideals from which much else good in the practice of law once flowed. Among them: the ideal of the seasoned lawyer as a wise counselor, or even per Abraham Lincoln's good counsel, a "peacemaker"; lawyers, in Professor Deborah Rhode's words, who have been "architects of a governmental structure that is a model for much of the world" and "leaders in virtually all major movements for social justice in the nation's history";[146] and countless lawyers in cities and towns across America, like those chronicled by Professor Walter Bennett and his students in their "oral histories," who "were living lives dedicated to a higher purpose, who loved what they were doing, and who found intellectual richness and creativity in lawyers' work."[147]

Having absorbed so much bad news about unhappy lawyers, so many lawyer jokes, so much "bitching and moaning," Professor Bennett reports "experienc[ing] something close to euphoria" when he discovered, *inter alia,* that there were still "lawyers and judges who were proud of being members of the profession, who felt that being a lawyer involved a deep moral commitment, that it was a position not only of prestige, but of honor."[148] In other words, Professor Bennett and his students discovered lawyers and judges who, consciously or unconsciously, had embraced law as a high calling.

Of course, if we take this higher road—if we embrace law as a calling "that involve[s] a deep moral commitment"[149]—there are a number of things we will instinctively understand we must *not* do. We will not, for example, lie or even make misleading representations to courts. We will not treat opposing counsel in a manner in which we would not want ourselves to be treated. We will not cheat or steal from our clients by doing unnecessary work or padding our billing records. And we will not take on work that we find morally offensive just because "everyone deserves a lawyer"—or, for that matter, because we could use the extra money.

Sadly, this has not been the direction of what we euphemistically (if not cynically) still call "legal ethics" in more recent decades. As Professor Glendon points out, we have come philosophical light years from the 1950s when corporate lawyers at least "sometimes [served as] 'conscience' to big business."[150] Putting the professionwide fear of making value judgments, God forbid, in historical perspective, Glendon observes:

> The first ABA Canons (adopted in 1908) held up a robust model of a lawyer who was no mere tool of the client: a lawyer "advances the honor of his profession and the best interests of his client when he renders service or gives advice tending to impress upon the client and his undertaking exact compliance with the strictest principles of moral law." In the 1960s, old-fashioned terms like "honor" and "principles of moral law" vanished, but the role of adviser and co-deliberator was still promoted: "A lawyer should exert his best efforts to insure that decisions of his client are made only after the client has been informed of relevant considerations. A lawyer ought to initiate this process if the client does not do so. Advice of a lawyer need not be confined to purely legal considerations. . . . In assisting his clients to reach a proper decision, it is often desirable for a lawyer to point out those factors which may lead to a decision that is morally just as well as legally permissible." In 1983, however, that mild encouragement to moral deliberation with clients was scrapped in favor of a provision that merely permits lawyers to refer to "relevant" factors: "In rendering advice, a lawyer may refer not only to law but to other considerations such as moral, economic, social and political factors, that may be relevant to the client's situation." Like Betty Crocker, the wise counselor has gotten slimmer over the years.[151]

In fact, as Professor Glendon later notes, "[t]he most hotly debated issue in connection with the 1983 Rules . . . was whether a lawyer should be required, rather than merely permitted, to disclose information he has reason to believe is necessary to prevent a client from causing *death* or *serious bodily harm* to another person."[152] Those advocating a morally based "do-the-right-thing" requirement soundly lost to what Professor Glendon describes as "the advocates of ironclad client confidentiality."[153]

With all due respect to the good men and women involved in the 1983 debate, that this was even a close call—death or serious bodily harm versus client confidentiality—is itself astounding. Can there be any question, when lawyer thinking strays that far from the "common good," why public opinion of lawyers has continued to plummet? Where are the ideals, or even what Dean Kronman calls "practical wisdom," in this bloodless, value-free calculus?

Dean Kronman is correct in connecting the collapse of historical ideals to the loss of "the professional self-confidence [they] once sustained."[154] It follows, if we are to have realistic hopes for regaining "professional self-confidence," that we must reaffirm ideals that transcend self-interest—including our individual and professionwide commitment to the "common good." We must not allow the legal profession to become an amoral, dollar-driven business; indeed, we should not be afraid to make value-based decisions or give advice grounded in moral conviction. In short, if we are to find fulfillment in the practice of law, we must take Step 10: We must embrace law as a high calling.

Step 11. Be generous with your time and money

G. K. Chesterton, the prolific British writer and polemicist, had a keen eye for the paradox. And no paradox lurking in life's lessons caught his eye more frequently than the inverse relationship between selfish materialism and happiness.

Most of us realize, at least in our better moments, that money and material acquisitions will not give us lasting satisfaction—but many, present company included, give it a good-faith effort! The lucky ones, like Brian Warnock,[155] ultimately realize that happiness lies elsewhere and, in fact, that devoting too much of our time and energy to acquiring will yield the opposite result.

We know, too, that the simple pronouncement of St. Paul that "it is more blessed to give than to receive"[156] is profoundly true, and that there is no "blessedness" (translated elsewhere as "happiness") in being a miser. Indeed, it is no coincidence that "miser" and "miserable" come from the same Latin root word.

Legal writing that attempts to make this point—that lawyers should be more generous with their time and money—tends to remain more narrowly focused on *pro bono* work. This is good counsel, as far as it goes, and more of us should strive to meet or exceed the ABA's suggested goal (at least 50 hours of *pro bono* work per year). As Professor

Rhode notes, "Few lawyers come close," and "[o]nly about a third of the nation's 500 largest firms have agreed to participate in the ABA Pro Bono Challenge, which requires a minimum annual contribution of three percent of the firm's total billable hours."[157] In his article "A Lawyer's Duty to Serve the Public Good," U.S. Circuit Judge Harry T. Edwards properly laments not only the reduction in pro bono practice, but also the declining number of law school graduates choosing public-service careers.[158]

But the declining commitment to pro bono work and public service is more derivative than central to the point we are trying to make here. In some ways—Chesterton would have loved this—our primary point here is more selfish, namely, that being generous with our time and money will make us feel better about our profession and our lives generally. In a word, giving generously will make us happier.

More central to our intended point is Steven Keeva's encouragement to develop a "helping heart."[159] He explains:

> In every tradition that emphasizes the importance of the inner life, compassion and service are held up as preeminent virtues. Those who, through the ages, have been revered for their wisdom and empathy—the Gandhis and the Martin Luther Kings of this world, to name but two recent examples—have often been people who believed that the very purpose of life is to be of service to others.
>
> Today's lawyers, being overwhelmingly inclined to minimize the importance of their inner experience, are more apt to see personal enrichment as their purpose, at least in their professional lives.[160]

To avoid suffering the misery of the miser, Keeva recommends a very simple exercise he calls "At Your Service":

> Freely giving your time and energy to others will repay you tenfold. You might consider looking for opportunities each week (or even every day) to perform random, anonymous acts of kindness. It's the holding of doors for others, picking up what someone else dropped, helping an elderly person across the street, or simply offering an encouraging smile that eventually help us to dissolve the boundaries that keep us feeling separate from one another. It will make you feel better and may come to have an impact on the way your practice law.[161]

Of course, the specific charity or "act of kindness" in which we engage is less important than developing an unselfish attitude. The essential point is, if fulfillment is one of our goals, after we provide for ourselves and our families, we will get more satisfaction out of generously giving than we will from hoarding.

Steven Keeva points to Mahatma Gandhi and Martin Luther King. The one who comes to my mind is Mother Teresa, the diminutive Yugoslavian peasant who moved to Calcutta to serve the poorest of the poor. Although most of us are not saints, we can all learn from those who are. And who could look at Mother Teresa—who died owning little more than her familiar blue and white sari and her rosary beads—and doubt that she had discovered a joy in life that eludes most contemporary Americans?

What Mother Teresa and others devoted to a charitable way of life discover is that it is indeed more blessed—happier—to give than to receive. Lawyers who are fortunate enough to make more money than they need should apply this important life lesson by taking Step 11, that is, by looking for opportunities to share their time, talents, and resources with others.

Step 12. Pace yourself for a marathon

If you have taken Steps 1 through 11, you are already well on your way to Step 12: pacing yourself "for a marathon." Clear priorities that balance work and personal lives, effective time management, healthy lifestyle habits and practices, resisting the most intrusive technology, dealing with excessive stress, and being more selective about clients and cases are each important steps toward our last goal: a sustainable pace.

Conversely, if you are working so many hours that you consistently come home exhausted (or so distracted you cannot enjoy family or friends outside of work); if you have not established clear priorities; if you are a poor time manager; if you seldom get a good aerobic workout; if your consumer spending is out of control; if you can never get away from the beeper, cell phone, and computer for "down time"; if stress is eating you up; or if the APC[162] of your client base is too high, you should probably deal with these issues first. Any one of these, left unattended for too long, is inconsistent with our ultimate goal, which is a healthy, well-balanced life.

As we consider Step 12—pacing yourself for a marathon—some of the previously made points warrant reiteration. Professor Schiltz's advice not to let yourself "be purchased at auction like a prize hog" or to "choose one law firm over another because of a $3,000 difference in starting salary"[163] is sound. Rather, make it clear from the outset—in your own mind first, and then with any prospective employer or partner—that only so much of you is "for sale." Make it clear that quality of life matters to you, that you intend to work hard and "pursue excellence" professionally, but not to sacrifice important relationships and other essential elements of a healthy, balanced life.

Speaking of pursuing excellence, there is a balance point here too. As noted by both Professor Dershowitz in *Letters to a Young Lawyer,*[164] and by Dr. Elwork in his book on stress management for lawyers,[165] striving for professional excellence is a good and worthy goal. In sharp and important contrast, trying to achieve perfection is not. Dershowitz offers a brief, two-page reflection he titles "The Perfect Is the Enemy of the Excellent" in which he observes that "[e]very book, painting, symphony, or speech could be improved. The search for perfection is illusory and has no end."[166]

He is absolutely correct, as is Dr. Elwork in concluding that "[s]ince perfection does not exist, perfectionists are doomed to be perpetually frustrated."[167] Pursuing excellence is consistent with a sustainable pace while the futile attempt to achieve perfection is not. "Given these distinctions, choosing to strive for excellence rather than perfection has important implications for how much job satisfaction you derive and how successful you become."[168] Strive for professional excellence, but be wary of any tendency you may have toward perfectionism.

Emotional health and balance is another important element of a sustainable pace. And because many of us depend upon warm relationships with children, and later grandchildren, for emotional strength, we should keep in mind San Francisco lawyer Michael Traynor's previously noted late-life observation "that the years with your children fly by in an instant."[169] Many will also want to take to heart Traynor's wise counsel, "[w]henever you can, [to] tell the god of money and the god of ambition, who is no less voracious, that you and your kids are going to fly a kite or build a snowman."[170]

The simple but important truth is that we are more likely to be emotionally balanced and healthy if we enjoy warm, loving relationships with those closest to us. This may not be spouses, children, or grandchildren in a particular case, of course, although for many it will be. But whoever they are, if those closest to us are having to remind us to "stop talking like a damn lawyer" too often, this may well be an area of our lives that needs attention.

Professor Dershowitz's previously noted observation that the wealthiest people tend to take the shortest vacations[171] brings us to another important point, if a sustainable pace is the goal. The advice here is about as straightforward as it gets: Take your vacation. All of it. You need it. The office and the practice will survive. And you will return refreshed, batteries recharged, with more enthusiasm and energy for your work. In fact, taking regular vacations will not only give you a sustainable pace, it will make you a better lawyer.

Finally, since we are using an athletic metaphor for what we are calling "Step 12," we will end with another exhortation to exercise regularly. It was no fluke that the North Carolina Bar Association's Quality of Life Task Force discovered, out of all the "lifestyle practices" examined, the highest correlation was between lawyers who got "regular exercise" and those who self-reported a sense of "subjective well-being."[172]

David B. Myers reviewed a number of psychological studies related to what made people "happy" in preparing to write his 1992 book, *The Pursuit of Happiness: Who Is Happy and Why*.[173] As summarized by Dr. Elwork, the number one factor noted as contributing to "happiness" was "physical health and fitness."[174] The bottom line: Lawyers who exercise regularly enjoy its stress-relieving effects, and are generally able to keep work pressures and demands in better perspective. If you have not done so already, make a commitment now to join them.

As we close this chapter, it is necessary to state what will be obvious to many readers, namely, that this "12-Step Program For Lawyers" is a career-long undertaking. Except for the extraordinarily well disciplined, and perhaps the most saintly, these are challenges and issues with which we can expect to struggle for the rest of our lives. But, thankfully, they are not impossible struggles, and if we diligently take these "steps," we can realistically expect to move closer to our goal: finding balanced success—and fulfillment—in the practice of law.

Notes

1. The author proposed abbreviated versions of a "12-step program" for lawyers, which included several systemic "steps" for firms, law schools, and the courts, in articles published in the 1990s by the *North Carolina Bar Journal*, the *South Carolina Lawyer*, and the ABA's *Law Practice Management* magazine. However,

this is the first published "12-step program" based solely on choices faced by the individual lawyer.

2. RICHARD M. WEAVER, IDEAS HAVE CONSEQUENCES (1948).
3. MARY ANN GLENDON, A NATION UNDER LAWYERS 3 (1994).
4. *See, e.g.,* SOL M. LINOWITZ (WITH MARTIN MAYER), THE BETRAYED PROFESSION: LAWYERING AT THE END OF THE TWENTIETH CENTURY (1994).
5. BENJAMIN SELLS, THE SOUL OF THE LAW: UNDERSTANDING LAWYERS AND THE LAW 34 (1994).
6. LAURENCE H. SILBERMAN, *Will Lawyering Strangle Democratic Capitalism?: A Retrospective,* 21 HARV. J.L. & PUB. POL'Y 607, 615 (1998).
7. JONATHAN FOREMAN, *My Life as an Associate,* CITY J., Winter 1997, at 89.
8. BRIAN WARNOCK, *A Professional Metamorphosis: From Workaholic to Part-Time Lawyer, in* BREAKING TRADITIONS: WORK ALTERNATIVES FOR LAWYERS 49 (Donna Killoughey ed., Amer. Bar Ass'n, 1993).
9. *Id.*
10. *Id.* at. 50.
11. MICHAEL TRAYNOR, *The Pursuit of Happiness,* 52 VAND. L. REV., May 1999, at 1025, 1030–31
12. *In* PROFESSOR PATRICK J. SCHILTZ'S provocative article discussed in chapters 2 and 3, *On Being a Happy, Healthy, and Ethical Member of an Unhappy, Unhealthy, and Unethical Profession,* 52 VAND. L. REV., May 1999, at 871, the author suggests that it is more than the desire for money that fuels the workaholism of many lawyers. Noting that lawyers will work absurdly long hours to earn incremental income they really do not need, Schiltz hypothesizes that for some it is a competitive game—akin to academic competitions, and then competitions for clerkships and the best jobs, at which they have excelled in the past—[a]nd money is how the score is kept in that game. *Id.* at 905.

    Professor Schiltz concludes:

    > It is not because these lawyers *need the money*. Any of these lawyers could lose every penny of his savings and *See* his annual income reduced by two-thirds and still live much more comfortably than the vast majority of Americans. What's driving these lawyers is the desire to *win the game.* These lawyers have spent their entire lives competing against others and measuring their worth by how well they do in the competitions. And now that they are working in a law firm, money is the way they keep score. Money is what tells them if they're more successful than the lawyer in the next office—or in the next office building—or in the next town. . . . For many, many lawyers, it's that simple.

    Id. at 906 (emphasis in original).
13. *Quoted in* DICK DAHL, *The Trouble With Lawyers,* BOSTON GLOBE MAG., Apr. 14, 1996, at 33.

14. ALAN DERSHOWITZ, LETTERS TO A YOUNG LAWYER (2001).
15. *Id.* at 33–35.
16. *Id.* at 34.
17. *Id.* at 35 (emphasis in original).
18. *Id.*
19. SCHILTZ, *supra* note 12, at 942.
20. *Id.*
21. *Id.*
22. *Id.*
23. ALEC MACKENZIE, THE TIME TRAP (1990).
24. *Id.* at 61.
25. MARGARET S. SPENCER, *Time Management, in* LIVING WITH THE LAW: STRATEGIES TO AVOID BURNOUT AND CREATE BALANCE 27 ((Julie M. Tamminen ed., Amer. Bar Ass'n 1997).
26. *Id.* at 28.
27. *Id.*
28. *Id.* (emphasis in original).
29. *Id.*
30. *Id.* at 28–29 (emphasis in original).
31. *Id.* at 29.
32. *Id.*
33. *Id.*
34. *Id.* (emphasis in original).
35. *Id.* (emphasis in original).
36. *Id.*
37. SPENCER, *supra* note 25, at 32.
38. *Id.* at 30.
39. *Id.*
40. *Id.*
41. *Id.*
42. AMIRAM ELWORK (WITH CONTRIBUTIONS BY DOUGLAS R. MARLOWE), STRESS MANAGEMENT FOR LAWYERS: HOW TO INCREASE PERSONAL AND PROFESSIONAL SATISFACTION IN THE LAW 139 (2d ed.1997).
43. *Id.*
44. *Id.* at 139–40.
45. SCHILTZ, *supra* note 12, at 880 n.60, citing North Carolina Bar Association's Report of the Quality of Life Task Force and Recommendations 4(1991), ABA Young Lawyers Div., The State of the Legal Profession 1990 51 (1991) (emphasis added).
46. SPENCER, *supra* note 25, at 34.
47. *Id.*

48. STEVEN KEEVA, TRANSFORMING PRACTICES: FINDING JOY AND SATISFACTION IN THE LEGAL LIFE (1999).
49. *Id.* at 28.
50. *Id.* at 47–48.
51. FOREMAN, *supra* note 7, at 91.
52. AMERICAN BAR ASS'N, THE PULSE OF THE PROFESSION 26 (November 22, 2000).
53. DEBORAH L. RHODE, IN THE INTERESTS OF JUSTICE: REFORMING THE LEGAL PROFESSION 32 (2000).
54. DERSHOWITZ, *supra* note 14, at 34.
55. *Id.* at 35.
56. *Id.*
57. The original Luddites were 19th century English workers who destroyed laborsaving machinery as a protest. They were pejoratively called Luddites in memory of Ned Ludd, an Englishman who had destroyed machinery for similar reasons in the 18th century. Today the term *Luddite* is used, inter alia, to refer to those who oppose technological change generally.
58. AMERICAN BAR ASS'N, *supra* note 52, at 32.
59. *See* note 57.
60. AMERICAN BAR ASS'N, *supra* note 52, at 32.
61. *Id.*
62. *Id.*
63. *Id.* at 40.
64. *Id.*
65. *Id.* at 63.
66. SCHILTZ, *supra* note 12, at 917.
67. *Id.*
68. *Id.*
69. *Id.* at 917–18.
70. *Id. at* 918.
71. *Id.*
72. *Id.*
73. *Id.* at 949.
74. *Id.* at 950.
75. AMERICAN BAR ASS'N, *supra* note 52, at 34.
76. ROGER E. SCHECHTER, *Changing Law Schools to Make Less Nasty Lawyers,* 10 GEO. J. LEGAL ETHICS, Winter 1997, at 367, 378. Schechter is a professor of law at George Washington University.
77. *Id.* at 378–79 (internal notes omitted).
78. *Id.* at 394 n.47.
79. *Id.* at 378, quoting PIERCE LIVELY, *A Tribute and Challenge to Exceptional Law Students* 77 KY. L.J. 759, 763 (1989).

80. AMERICAN BAR ASS'N, *supra* note 52, at 34.
81. *Id.*
82. *Id.*
83. GLENDON, *supra* note 3, at 61.
84. *See* the text at notes 65–73.
85. SOL M. LINOWITZ (WITH MARTIN MAYER), THE BETRAYED PROFESSION: LAWYERING AT THE END OF THE TWENTIETH CENTURY 31 (1994).
86. *Id.*, quoting ROY GRUTMAN & BILL THOMAS, LAWYERS AND THIEVES 28 (1990).
87. *Id.*
88. WALT BACHMAN, LAW V. LIFE: WHAT LAWYERS ARE AFRAID TO SAY ABOUT THE LEGAL PROFESSION 135 (1995).
89. *Id.*
90. LINOWITZ, *supra* note 85, at 30.
91. *Id.* at 31.
92. *Id.* (emphasis in original).
93. *Id.* at 34–35.
94. *Id.*, quoting HARRY WEINSTEIN, *Attorney Liability in the Savings and Loan Crisis,* 1993 U. OF ILL. L. REV. 53, 61 (1993).
95. BACHMAN, *supra* note 88, at 21.
96. AMERICAN BAR ASS'N, *supra* note 52, at 30.
97. *See* KEEVA, *supra* note 48, at 198–201.
98. AMERICAN BAR ASS'N, *supra* note 52, at 30.
99. *See* Matthew 5:45.
100. AMERICAN BAR ASS'N, *supra* note 52, at 30.
101. *Id.*
102. *Quoted in* KEEVA, *supra* note 48, at 198.
103. *Id.* at 198–99.
104. *Id.* at 199.
105. *Id.*
106. BACHMAN, *supra* note 88, at 115.
107. *Id.*
108. *Id.* at 119–22.
109. *Id.* at 122.
110. *Id.* at 123.
111. *Id.*
112. *Id.*
113. *Id.*
114. KEEVA, *supra* note 48, at 200–01.
115. *Id.* at 201.
116. SELLS, *supra* note 5, at 177.
117. *Id.* at 176–77 (emphasis in original).
118. *Id.* at 176.

119. *Id.* at 178.
120. *Id.* at 178–79.
121. WALTER BENNETT, THE LAWYER'S MYTH: REVIVING IDEALS IN THE LEGAL PROFESSION ix, 2 (2001).
122. *See* text in chapter 2 at note 113.
123. GEORGE W. KAUFMAN, THE LAWYER'S GUIDE TO BALANCING LIFE AND WORK: TAKING THE STRESS OUT OF SUCCESS 13 (1999).
124. *Id.*
125. *Id.*
126. STEVEN KEEVA, *A Symphony of Silence,* CAL. L. WK., Aug. 9, 1999, at 31.
127. *Id.*
128. *Id.*
129. *Id.*
130. KAUFMAN, *supra* note 123, at 52.
131. *Id.*
132. *Id.*
133. *Id.* at 57.
134. *Id.* at 78.
135. *Id.* at 81.
136. *Id.* at 154.
137. PETER KUTULAKIS, *Stress Management Checklists, in* LIVING WITH THE LAW: STRATEGIES TO AVOID BURNOUT AND CREATE BALANCE 81–83 (Julie M. Tamminen ed., Amer. Bar Ass'n 1997).
138. ELWORK, *supra* note 42.
139. KUTULAKIS, *supra* note 137.
140. *Id.; accord* ELWORK, *supra* note 42, at 44.
141. KAUFMAN, *supra* note 123, at 127–31.
142. ANTHONY T. KRONMAN, THE LOST LAWYER: FAILING IDEALS OF THE LEGAL PROFESSION 1–2 (1993).
143. *Id.* at 2.
144. *Id.*
145. *Id.* at 2–3.
146. RHODE, *supra* note 53, at 3.
147. BENNETT, *supra* note 121, at 6.
148. *Id.*
149. *Id.*
150. GLENDON, *supra* note 3, at 75.
151. *Id.* at 79–80 (internal notes omitted).
152. *Id.* at 81.
153. *Id.*
154. KRONMAN, *supra* note 142, at 3.
155. *See* text at notes 8–10.
156. Acts 20:35.

157. RHODE, *supra* note 53, at 37.
158. HARRY T. EDWARDS, *A Lawyer's Duty to Serve the Public Good,* 65 N.Y.U. L. Rev. 1148, 1152–54 (1990).
159. KEEVA, *supra* note 48, at 133.
160. *Id.*
161. *Id.* at 134.
162. *See* text at notes 106–113.
163. *See* text at notes 19–22.
164. DERSHOWITZ, *supra* note 14, at 77–78.
165. ELWORK, *supra* note 42, at 152–53.
166. DERSHOWITZ, *supra* note 14, at 77–78.
167. ELWORK, *supra* note 42, at 153.
168. *Id.*
169. TRAYNOR, *supra* note 11, at 1030–31.
170. *Id.*
171. DERSHOWITZ, *supra* note 14, at 35.
172. *See* text in Step 4, *supra.*
173. DAVID G. MYERS, THE PURSUIT OF HAPPINESS: WHO IS HAPPY AND WHY (1992).
174. ELWORK, *supra* note 42, at 157.

CHAPTER 5

Help Wanted: Law Schools, Firms, and Bar Organizations

If the legal profession is ever to command the public respect it enjoyed in better days, and if what we have called LawyerLife is to be restored to health, it will take more than individual lawyers making the good choices commended in the last chapter. It will take these individual "steps" to be sure, but it will also take a concerted effort by the key institutions involved in the education, training, and governance of the nation's lawyers: law schools, firms, and bar organizations.

Law Schools

Thinking logically, one might assume that the place to begin a coordinated effort to produce healthy, ethical, well-balanced lawyers would be in the schools where they receive their initial education and training. But those of us who graduated more than 20 years ago and have not kept up with trends and developments in legal education may be more than a little surprised by the resistance—or, more likely, the indifference—we find in many law faculty. In the vernacular, many really don't give a damn about how it goes in the contemporary practice. So the first hurdle in engaging law schools in our struggle is to convince a critical mass of law faculty and administrators that they have an obligation to care about the life and professional world into which their students are graduating.

In fact, there has been increasing commentary on this problem, which U.S. Circuit Judge Harry T. Edwards has called "the growing disjunction between legal education and the legal profession."[1] Interestingly, the most intense criticism is coming from academics at the most elite schools, perhaps emboldened by former Harvard President Derek Bok's sweeping criticism of legal education, published 20 years ago under the title, "A Flawed System."[2] Although the burden of Bok's critique was the overemphasis on conflict in the law school curriculum, and the relative neglect of "the gentler arts of reconciliation and accommodation,"[3] his frontal attack on the status quo opened the academic door to other broad criticism.

The reader has been introduced to perhaps the most scholarly of these broad critiques of legal education: Yale Law School Dean Anthony T. Kronman's 1993 book, *The Lost Lawyer: Failing Ideals of the Legal Profession*.[4] Although his analysis is deeply and densely philosophical—chronicling, for example, how the law-and-economics and critical legal studies movements have supplanted the more practical focus of law professors of yesteryear—Dean Kronman's essential application does not require a background in philosophy or jurisprudence to understand. Law schools "now encourage a style of scholarly work," Kronman concludes, "that is increasingly remote from—even hostile to—the concerns of practicing lawyers."[5]

Harvard Law Professor Mary Ann Glendon made similar points in her book published the next year, *A Nation Under Lawyers*. In a chapter titled "The New Academy," she scores contemporary law professors for their disdainful "attitudes toward the practice of law, especially private practice."[6] "Such attitudes not only have widened the separation between the academy and the bar," Professor Glendon warns, "they have also created an unfortunate gap between the interests of professors and the concerns of students."[7]

According to George Washington University Law Professor Roger E. Schechter, "the perception of a profession gone awry" simply does not come up much in "routine discussion" among law faculty.[8]

"It is rare . . . to hear of the troubles that beset the profession in . . . the faculty lounges," Professor Schechter reports. "It is even more rare to hear conversations about the connections between the structure of legal education and the condition—both actual and perceived—of the profession."[9] Writing in 1999, Professor Patrick J. Schiltz, then an Associate Professor of Law at Notre Dame Law School,[10] had no doubt why subjects related to lawyer unhappiness rarely come up among faculty. "[M]any law professors—at least those teaching at the 50 or so schools that consider themselves to be in the 'Top 20'—do not care much about lawyers," Professor Schiltz bluntly concludes. "Increasingly, faculties of elite schools and aspiring elite schools consist of professors who have not practiced law, who have little interest in teaching students to practice law, and who pay scant attention to the work of practicing lawyers."[11]

There are two fundamental reasons why "[l]aw professors must begin to conceive of themselves as members of the legal profession as well as the academic profession,"[12] as former University of North Carolina Law Professor Walter Bennett expresses the essential need. First, the law school years are simply the most logical time to build the foundation and think through the personal commitments necessary to achieve a balanced, healthy professional life. And second, there is growing evidence that many of the problems with which contemporary lawyers struggle—including depression, skewed priorities, difficulty in maintaining intimate relationships, and inordinate financial pressures—actually have their origin in the law school experience.

Writing in the *Journal of Law and Health* in 1999, Florida State Law Professor Lawrence S. Krieger laments "the inability of legal education to consistently graduate lawyers who are happy, balanced, and who would naturally aspire to professionalism in its most exalted sense."[13] Noting studies showing "lawyers and law students are much more likely than the general population to experience emotional distress, depression, anxiety, addictions, and other related mental, physical, and social problems,"[14] Krieger is one law professor who looks for ways to communicate life-sustaining truths to his students. In an article titled "What We're Not Telling Law Students—and Lawyers—That They Really Need to Know: Some Thoughts-in-Action Toward Revitalizing the Profession From Its Roots," Krieger urges law faculty to find ways to teach their students, *inter alia*:

- that their aspirations for honors and high achievement are valuable only in the context of a balanced, happy life;
- that they can have good lives as lawyers if they act according to their conscience, their deep personal values, and their ideals; and [conversely]
- that they *cannot* have good lives as lawyers if they do *not* act according to their conscience, deep personal values, and ideals.[15]

Professor Krieger, in his commendable passion to help students achieve "meaningful and healthful lives as lawyers," also makes what is perhaps an even more foundational point when he instructs his students "that, as attorneys, their best personal attributes are more important than their best skills or performances."[16]

Although there is need for further study, Stanford Law Professor Deborah L. Rhode's summary of the available research on psychological distress among law students is accurate. "Although the psychological profile of entering law students matches that of the public generally," Professor Rhode reports, "an estimated 20 to 40 percent leave with some psychological dysfunction including depression, substance abuse, and various stress-related disorders."[17]

Professor Rhode's summary is certainly consistent with the most significant studies of law student "psychological distress," conducted at the University of Arizona Law School by three professors of psychology and a professor of psychiatry in the mid-1980s.[18] As reported in a 1986 article published by the American Bar Foundation, the students entered law school with "psychopathological symptom responses that were similar to the normal population" but by the second semester of their first year a significant percentage had "symptom levels [that were] significantly elevated."[19] Specifically, the authors reported that 20 to 40 percent of the law students participating in the study "reported . . . significantly elevated [psychopathological] symptoms, including obsessive-compulsive behavior, interpersonal sensitivity, anxiety, hostility, paranoid ideation, and psychoticism (social alienation and isolation)."[20]

Of course, even those of us who attended law school in an earlier generation recall how stressful the first year can be, and a certain amount of pressure and stress is unavoidable. Indeed, before ideological movements began to dominate law faculty, there were still the Professor Kingsfields (of "Paper Chase" fame) bent on converting our "minds filled with mush" to the logical, analytical organs we would need to become successful lawyers. I recall my wife being called on by a particularly cruel law professor in our first-year torts class (in 1973). As she stood and closed her book, per her professor's command, she simultaneously knocked the book off the desk on the back of the student in front of her and nervously lost her voice. Utterly humiliated, that was the last law school class she ever attended, opting for a kinder, gentler position in a corporate trust department.

And that is fine. No one is suggesting that law school or the practice of law should always be a kind or gentle experience, or that either can or should be freed from all stress or pressure. But when studies show that a significant percentage of lawyers are clinically depressed or even suicidal, and that the "psychopathological symptoms" that lead to these conditions (and undermine professional fulfillment, destroy relationships, and on and on) begin in law school, it is simply inexcusable for law faculty and administrators not to care. It is also inexcusable for law faculty to tear down ideals and moral values students have developed during their first 22 years (or more) of life, and to care so little about what, if anything, fills the created void.

Professor Walter Bennett, recalling his own moral confusion as a first-year law student at the University of Virginia in 1969, routinely asked students in his professional responsibility classes to write short papers on "The Moral Reasons (if any) Why I Came to Law School" and "The Effects of Law School upon My Personal Value System."[22] He did this, wisely, not to tell the students what their morals or values should be, but to engage them in healthy introspection so that they might avoid the "abiding cynicism" that can all too easily become a "byproduct" of "learning to think like a lawyer."[23]

Professor Bennett makes another important, if subtle, point that should be emphasized. Aware that students often arrive at law school with "morally limited . . . stories," that is, with ideals and values that need to be challenged, refashioned, or even replaced, Bennett's essential concern is that the law school experience not thwart or stunt the student's capacity for moral reasoning. In other words, he sees "the real danger . . . not so much in the change in one's moral story about oneself, but in the damage to one's capacity for moral growth."[24] Understanding the need to avoid simplistic moralizing, Bennett correctly concludes that *continued moral growth* is what "gives purpose and definition to lawyers' work," and therefore, that "discourse in the greater moral context" should be "a central part of legal education."[25]

As it turns out, many law professors are even more squeamish about teaching the practical skills necessary for successful lawyering than they are about moral reasoning. "Today's law students can graduate well versed in postmodern literary theory but ill equipped to draft a document," Professor Rhode properly complains. "They may learn to 'think like a lawyer' but not to make a living at it."[26] Indeed, unless they get it from practical clerking experience, many law students graduate with no idea how to conduct an interview, counsel a client, negotiate, or to engage in any number of other need-to-know practical skills. "Law schools claim, above all else, that they teach students how to 'think like a lawyer.' In fact, they often teach how to think like a law professor, in a form distanced and detached from human contexts."[27]

It is entirely understandable that law faculty and administrators resist pressures to become mere vocational schools. That is as it should be. However, the pendulum has swung too far and proper balance has not been struck when so many young lawyers are graduating, as the ABA Pulse Study put it, without "any real sense of what the practice of law is really like nor how to execute even the most basic tasks."[28] This causes many young lawyers to feel overwhelmed and propels others into the depression they have successfully avoided up to that point. "I really liked law school," one new lawyer told an ABA focus group in Chicago, "but it doesn't prepare you at all."[29] "It's scary," another new lawyer told the focus group convened in Sacramento. "I think that's [from] where most of the stress comes. . . . "[30] Or, as an older lawyer in Birmingham, Alabama bluntly put it, "You go to law school, and you learn how to look up the law, but you go to work, and you feel dumb as a post. You don't know how to practice law."[31]

The ABA Pulse Study, published in November 2000, also identified as a significant concern of younger lawyers the financial pressures caused by student loan indebtedness—another problem with origins in the law school years, although one that is more attributable to the decisions of individual students (and their parents) than to law school faculty or administrators. According to best-guess estimates, "[r]oughly one in three law students graduates with no student loan debt. Of the remaining two-thirds, the average loan debt upon graduation is $40,000."[32] The average loan debt for University of North Carolina Law School, "one of the least expensive state law schools in the country, exceeded $30,000.00" several years ago,[33] and is probably not atypical for graduates of state schools. And apparently it is "not uncommon for a new lawyer to owe more than $100,000 for combined college and law school expenses" upon graduation.[34]

Not surprisingly, once they graduate (if not before) young lawyers begin to realize the real-life consequences of beginning professional life with this much debt. As Professor Rhode notes, indebted young lawyers "are registering increasing regrets about choosing a profession in which they can't reconcile their debt with their dreams."[35] Young lawyers who participated in the ABA focus groups certainly did. For some, like the "New Bar Admittee" in Chicago who graduated with significant debt, the issue becomes "doing what I really enjoy" versus "paying off debt for a while."[36] For others, the justified pride and sense of accomplishment that should attend graduation and passing the bar is overshadowed by a sense of being "trapped into staying in a job they dislike simply to pay off loan commitments."[37]

Responsibility for the student loan debt many students assume cannot be fairly attributed to policies or decisions of law faculty or administrators—at least not primarily. But that does not mean law faculty and administrators need show no concern about seeds sown on their watch that appear to be blossoming, increasingly, into professional discontent. Indeed, there may be a moral obligation to advise law students that the financial obligations they have assumed may be inconsistent with the reasons they pursued a career in law in the first place.

What practical lessons do we take from these observations about the negative consequences of student loan indebtedness? First, if you are a law student (or prospective law student) who has not yet made the decision to incur substantial debt, think long and hard before you do. Consider the alternatives: less-expensive schools, schools offering nonloan financial aid, working and saving for a year or two before law school, and other sources of funding. Parents with the ability to help their children graduate with reduced or no debt would be well advised to do so. Making it financially in today's world, particularly if obligations include supporting a family, are difficult enough without adding a gargantuan student loan debt to the equation. If parents of law students are looking for that "very special" thing to do for their son or daughter, this may be it. If you can, help your child graduate with little or no debt.

Law school faculty and administrators, especially when asked, should be honest about the real-life consequences of student loan debt—even if it means some students choose to attend other schools. Efforts should be made to present this message clearly to students, for example, through invited speakers, available literature, and individual counseling. And as Professor Roger Schechter urges in "Changing Law Schools to Make Less Nasty Lawyers," this best-interest-of-the-law-student approach to student debt would also commend an effective loan-forgiveness program for those who choose lower-paying public employment after graduation.[38]

An effective loan-forgiveness program speaks to two issues of concern in the contemporary practice: financial pressures caused, in part, by substantial student loans, and the decreasing number of law school graduates choosing public service careers. And in addition to the most basic element of any loan-forgiveness program—excusing some portion of the accumulated debt for each year spent in public employment—I suggest another: allowing graduates who take public service positions full access to the school's career placement services for a limited period, say five or six years, following graduation. Some undoubtedly will remain in public service careers, and more will give it a try if their decision is not seen at the outset as irreversible.

Assuming a critical mass of law faculty and administrators can be persuaded to care about the real-life experience of their graduates, Professor Schechter makes a number of other practical suggestions that are, if nothing more, excellent food for thought. Organizing his suggestions around three areas of concern—"the litigation crisis," "the civility crisis," and "the public service crisis"—Schechter suggests several law school responses to each and then concludes by incorporating his suggestions into a reformed law school curriculum.[39]

Regarding "the litigation crisis," which is probably more responsible for the negative public opinion of lawyers than any other single factor, Schechter suggests a required first-year course "in mediation or a more general alternative dispute resolution course," as well as "a course that explicitly inquires into both the economic and psychological costs of litigation and its effect on productivity and social tensions."[40] The hope, of course, is that presenting these counterbalancing truths to impressionable law students will encourage them later to "dissuad[e] a client from filing a dubious lawsuit."[41]

In response to "the civility crisis"—evidenced, for example, by lawyers "refusing to return phone calls, grant routine extensions of deadlines, or even shake hands in court," and occasionally by "more abrasive and hostile behaviors such as vulgarity and name calling"[42]—Professor Schecher's suggestions are equally plainspoken and practical. First, he encourages law faculty to continue the move away from "socratic abusiveness" (think Kingsfield) in favor of "a kinder and gentler teaching style."[43] Beyond that, he advocates law teachers looking for opportunities "to inject affirmative sermons on civility and professionalism into all courses"; more formal teacher-training programs in which law teachers are specifically instructed on "the negative effects of sarcasm and bullying"; and the development of "materials addressing civility issues" to which all students would be exposed before graduation.[44]

To deal with "the public service crisis," in addition to the loan forgiveness program, Professor Schechter recommends "[a]doption of a mandatory *pro bono* requirement under which each student would have to perform a certain amount of free legal work for indigent clients before graduation"; and "[d]evelopment of specific courses devoted to problems of indigents such as consumer law, landlord and tenant law or poverty law, coupled with a requirement that every student take one such course before graduation."[46] He also makes two recommendations likely to be more controversial and/or difficult to implement, namely, a mandatory *pro bono* requirement "for the faculty that would obligate each full-time professor to perform a specified amount of direct client work for indigents each year," and pushing back the time in the school year when private firms are allowed on campus to conduct interviews.[47]

Putting Professor Schechter's suggestions into a curriculum, he suggests, "would look something like this":[48]

FIRST YEAR

Fall Semester	**Spring Semester**
Contracts (4)	Property (4)
Torts (4)	Criminal Law & Procedure (4)
Dispute Resolution I (3)	Dispute Resolution II (3)
Professionalism I (2)	Professionalism II (2)
Legal Research & Writing (2)	Counseling Competition (2)

SECOND YEAR

Fall Semester	**Spring Semester**
Corporations (4)	Evidence (4)
Constitutional Law (4)	*Pro Bono* Requirement (3)
Problems of the Indigent (3)	Electives (8)

THIRD YEAR

Fall Semester	**Spring Semester**
Journal Participation (2)	Journal Participation (2)
Electives (13)	Electives (13)

Although not explicitly stated, the numbers in parentheses after the courses apparently represent the proposed credits each would carry. Not having run it by any of my law professor acquaintances, I do not know how law faculty or administrators would respond to the suggested reforms, which border on the radical, but I suspect there will at least be a significant minority who will welcome the fresh air they represent.

As we consider what law schools can and should do to remedy problems in contemporary practice, it might be helpful to reflect for a moment on how legal education has changed and evolved through the years. "All that is necessary for a [law] student," Thomas Jefferson opined, "is access to a library and directions in what order the books are to be read."[49] More than half a century later, in 1858, Abraham Lincoln's prescription was pretty much the same. "[T]he cheapest, best way" to prepare for a legal career," Lincoln wrote, was to "read Blackstone's *Commentaries*, Chitty's *Pleadings,* Greenleaf's *Evidence,* Story's *Equity* and *Equity Pleading,* get a license, and go to the practice and still keep reading."[50] According to Professor Lawrence M. Friedman, the nation's leading legal historian, this continued to be an accepted path into the profession in 1900, when "[n]o state made a law degree, or a college degree, absolutely necessary for admission to the bar. . . . "[51]

Not only did "reading for the bar"—and, for the lucky ones, apprenticeship to a successful lawyer—remain an accepted pathway to practice into the twentieth century, but the "case method of teaching law" predominated only in a minority of the 95 or so law schools that did exist.[52] Many of these schools had a local focus, the rise of "national law schools" studying majority and minority rules being yet another twentieth-century innovation.[53] "To be sure, few schools that taught local law taught it as anything better than tricks of the lawyers trade, nuts and bolts of practical information."[54] No one is advocating that we go back to that. Rather, with legal education lately on a fast evolutionary track, the point here is that there is nothing sacrosanct about its current condition.

Thankfully, a growing number of law faculty and administrators are noticing the blind spots and imbalances in the current law school curriculum and experience. We have been introduced in these pages to a number of them, and we have seen that they hail from law schools ranging from the "elite" to state schools to those generally described as "regional." In fact, some of the latter are doing much of the best work in this area. Campbell University's School of Law in Buies Creek, North Carolina—which graduates a higher percentage of students who pass the state bar exam almost every year than does nearby (and "elite") Duke University—has emphasized quality-of-life issues in its curriculum and program for over a decade. Northeastern and Suffolk University law schools, both in Boston, are two other "regional" schools that have creatively addressed the post-graduation happiness and professional fulfillment of their students.[55]

Bravo to these academic pioneers, individual and institutional—and let's have many more of them in the near future. Individual lawyers must ultimately establish priorities and make good choices if professional fulfillment is to be achieved. But how much more likely that would be if these issues were framed, and necessary commitments thought through, during the formative law school years. Indeed, for many lawyers the presence or absence of this message in law school will be *the* material factor determining whether they ultimately find—or lose—their way.

Law Firms

However well or poorly law school has prepared us, the next step for most graduates is a law firm. It is in the firm that the lessons learned in law school, and any commitments we have made, will be tried and tested. For most of us, the firm will become the single greatest influence on how we practice law, and ultimately on whether we find it professionally fulfilling.

The most important lessons "taught" by a first employer come not in words or policies, but in the lives of the lawyers—associates and partners—who are already there. Their actions, their balance or lack of balance, their personalities and character will speak volumes to the new associate. The importance that their collective message be positive and hopeful cannot be overemphasized.

As we have seen, the number-one complaint of unhappy lawyers appears to be the incredibly long hours many are working. What they expected to be stimulating and exciting, many lawyers find, has become a terrible grind. To again paraphrase the nursery truism, all work and no play make dull men and women. And Sol Linowitz is correct: Those who consistently neglect all but their work lives will, paradoxically, also become less valuable to their clients.

Translation: Law firms should set reasonable billable-hours requirements—if, indeed, they set any at all—and be concerned enough to intervene when individual lawyers begin to lose balance. However much money its "human capital" is bringing in, a conscientious firm will never knowingly permit its lawyers to fall into unhealthy workaholism.

There are a growing number of firms of all sizes that are realizing this. Charlotte-based Kennedy Covington Lobdell & Hickman, one of the preeminent firms in the southeast (with about 170 lawyers in four locations), recently spent a year and a half developing a "mission statement" and "statement of core values." Using successful companies as models, partners, associates, and staff worked together to articulate and record the foundational principles and values for which they collectively hope their firm will stand. Managing partners Charles ("Buddy") DuBose and Henry ("Hank") Flint guided the project to completion, and now refer to these documents regularly in making a wide variety of decisions affecting the firm.

One of the beneficial results of this process was a new compensation system, governed by a democratically elected committee, that takes into consideration the firm's well-balanced "mission" and "values" in deciding how the money is divided up each year. In addition to the usual considerations (fees billed and collected, and business developed, for example), the compensation committee recognizes that "[c]ontributing time and resources to [the legal] profession and the communities in which [they] live is an essential part of the firm's mission," and keeps clearly in mind that its "core values" include "[w]orking as a team"; "[m]aintaining a culture of mutual trust, loyalty, and respect"; "[t]aking the time to care for, and enjoy the company of, [one another]"; and "the need for balance in each individual's professional and personal life." Thus, mentoring younger lawyers, engaging in charitable and civic activities, doing *pro bono* work, and spending time with friends and family are not regarded as tolerable distractions—assuming, of course, billable hours requirements are met or exceeded—but as an essential part of *the firm's* priority business.

We should be careful when we encounter horror stories—like "partners giv[ing] assignments to associates on Christmas Eve with the clear expectation that they be completed the next day" or "lawyers work[ing] all night to complete a rush assignment only to find the next morning the assigning partner wouldn't be in that day"[56]—not to assume they are the norm. Tyrants, like the partners Jonathan Foreman and his fellow associates nicknamed "Dave the Barracuda" and "Caligula,"[57] exist, but they are on the extreme end of any spectrum. And in contrast to these extremes, most partners would probably affirm, at least in their better and wiser moments, the importance of a healthy, balanced life. With a little luck and the right facilitator, they might even label it a "core value."

Hindi Greenberg, who held a wide range of legal positions (judicial clerk, litigator in a large and later a small firm, and in-house counsel) after graduating from law school in 1974, founded Lawyers in Transition[58] in 1985. Described by the *Los Angeles Times* as the "Ann Landers for Lawyers,"[59] Greenberg's San Francisco–based company promotes "career satisfaction for lawyers in and out of the law . . . and provides law firms with remedies for associate dissatisfaction."[60] In a chapter (of an ABA publication) titled "How to Create a Desirable Work Environment for Associates," Ms. Greenberg suggests the following "composite wish list":

- To be fully integrated into the law firm, treated with respect for past accomplishments, and given support and effective feedback for future efforts;
- To receive continuing education, both within and outside of the firm; interesting work, with increasing responsibility as ability warrants; humane and fair working arrangements; good pay; tolerable hours; and additional benefits and bonuses;
- To be treated as individuals, even allowed to market a specialized practice in a more entrepreneurial style; [and]
- To identify with the compassionate values of the firm as demonstrated by *pro bono* commitments, training programs, employee diversity, reasonable billable hours, and part-time and family-leave policies.[61]

The bottom line, according to Greenberg, who "based [her suggestions] on . . . conversations with thousands of *unhappy* lawyers," is that "[a]ssociates want a balance between professional and personal goals, between economic success and personal satisfaction. A consuming career is no longer enough."[62]

If unreasonably long hours is the number one complaint of unhappy lawyers—and it clearly is—for younger lawyers, the unavailability of more experienced partners to guide and train them is perhaps a close second. The ABA Pulse Study concluded that "a lack of mentoring the next generation of lawyers" was the profession's "Pressure Point #3."[63] As the Study described the problem, "[m]entoring younger associates is falling victim to the pressures of cost and time; this, in turn, often means younger associates are left to their own devices, leading many to feel frustrated and isolated."[64] A law firm that wants to keep its associates, maximizing their productivity in the early years and developing those who are capable into solid partners, must *not* neglect its obligation to mentor.

As Professor Bennett notes, not too many years ago "professional mentoring by elders was the primary method by which initiates entered into professional status in the law."[65] And Bennett is also correct that restoring "professional ideals" will require us to "resurrect the individual obligation of bar members to educate initiates (and other members of the bar generally) in professional values and aspirations."[66] In a word, we must realize, as the forward-thinking Kennedy Covington firm has, that mentoring is as valuable and essential to a law firm's well-being as are collectible fees and new business.

And finally, the law firm that cares about its partners and associates—which, after all, is in its own long-term best interest—must address "stress." We will acknowledge again that law practice has never been a nine-to-five job. No matter how hard a particular firm works to keep reasonable hours or to ensure a humane, balanced work environment, at times the practice of law will be highly stressful. The jealous mistress—or master—will get the upper hand. More firms must learn to recognize the debilitating effects of prolonged, excessive stress, and take the necessary steps to deal with it.

The good news is the ample and growing expertise, some of which is tailored specifically for lawyers and law firms, to help us reduce and manage stress. We have met a number of these experts in this book; their writing has been cited, their services recommended. Many more who have not been mentioned offer services on a local or regional basis, and can be located by concerned lawyers or law firms with minimal effort.

Preston K. Munter, M.D., a psychiatrist who has served as a consultant to the ABA, the Boston Bar Association, and many law firms, sums up many of the steps law firms can and should take in "Law Firm Policies and Procedures to Reduce Stress."[67] Dr. Munter lays out, in a logical and readable style, what he has learned from countless hours helping lawyers identify common sources of unnecessary, unhealthy stress. More importantly, he prescribes specific steps, policies, and strategies to reduce stress to levels generally considered reasonable and manageable.

In summary, the law firm that hopes to thrive in the future cannot neglect the health and well-being of its partners, associates, or staff. Conversely, those short-sighted firms that conduct their affairs as though only money matters will find themselves less able to retain the very source of their profits. This is true because, thanks be to God, even "human capital" still have feet.

The Organized Bar

Of the three institutions highlighted in this chapter—law school, firms, and the organized bar—it is the bar that has most consistently been there for lawyers in distress. And for the most part, help from the bar has come through expanding the focus and committing increased resources to "lawyer assistance programs" (LAPs) and to various efforts promoting "professionalism."

Traditionally, the emphasis of the bar's "lawyer assistance programs" was on helping those who developed alcohol-related problems, although most expanded in the 1970s to 1980s to address "substance abuse" generally. As studies and surveys began to show that many lawyers were unhappy professionally, and a certain number even clinically depressed, bar initiatives further expanded their scope to encompass these problems. Those who have taken an active part in the organized bar's response to these issues and problems deserve hearty commendation for their compassion and foresight.

Similarly, the bar's emphasis on "professionalism" was traditionally limited to applying the Code of Professional Responsibility, somewhat euphemistically referred to in simpler times as "ethics." Again, bar leaders are to be commended for realizing that the Code of Professional Responsibility was an inadequate response to growing public disrespect or rising lawyer discontent, and broadening their "professionalism" initiatives accordingly.

Of course, some bars have done more than others, and there is room for improvement and a need for further expansion in almost all. Continuing Legal Education (CLE) programs that emphasize balance or quality of life issues are more readily approved for credit by some bar organizations than others. Professionalism efforts of some state and local bars remain too narrowly focused. More could be done to help law schools prepare students for the real-life pressures of practice, and more effective resources could be developed for firm partners who will accede to this responsibility upon graduation. The primary emphasis here must be positive, however; the trends in the voluntary bar response to the concerns raised in this book are most definitely in the right direction.

The Virginia Bar Association (VBA), which in 2001 created a new Law Practice Management Division, is a good example of this positive and hopeful trend. Writing in *The Virginia Bar Association News Journal*, Chair Heman A. Marshall III explains that the new division—only the second created in the VBA's long history—grew out of the perceived need "as an element of the promotion of professionalism . . . to focus on the balance between a successful and rewarding practice and other lifestyle issues such as health, family relationships, and intellectual development."[69] Marshall reports that by expanding what was previously a "section" into a "division," the VBA "will add equal emphasis on the individual and personal aspects of law practice management, such as personal time management, professional skills development, personal marketing, achieving an appropriate practice/lifestyle balance, and promoting overall professionalism."[70]

As noted in chapter 2, the South Carolina Bar is also doing exemplary work to address lawyer balance, and health generally, under the broader rubric of "professionalism."[71] Under the effective leadership of J. Robert Turnbull, Jr., the South Carolina Bar's "Lawyers Helping Lawyers Program" works with the University of South Carolina School of Law's "Nelson Mullins Riley & Scarborough Center on Professionalism" to provide a wide range of educational and confidential personal services.[72] Reorganized with increased emphasis and resources in 2001, Lawyers Helping Lawyers has four stated purposes:

1. to protect the interests of the general public and clients from harm caused by lawyers and judges impaired by substance abuse and/or depression;
2. to protect the integrity of the legal profession from harm caused by lawyers and judges impaired by substance abuse and/or depression;
3. to educate the bench and bar about the causes and remedies for substance abuse and/or depression within the profession; and
4. to provide help to lawyers and judges who suffer from substance abuse and/or depression.[73]

Writing in the *South Carolina Lawyer*, Turnbull credits the broad-based governance of the newly organized initiative, which is led by an 11-member commission and actively advised by a "Committee . . . made up of more than 45 active and retired members of the South

Carolina Bar from throughout the state."[74] Not surprisingly, the statewide leadership of this lawyer-assistance program has resulted in broader-than-average awareness of their availability and more resources at the local level for lawyers who need their confidential services.

The Nelson Mullins Riley & Scarborough Center on Professionalism at the University of South Carolina School of Law is doing pioneer work in several respects. First, there is the work itself: A large project by any measure, the center's initial mission was to identify and provide resources to professors in every law school in the country who teach or are interested in "professionalism" (broadly defined). Second, there is the national accessibility of the information through the center's web site, which also includes a rich array of recommended resources, relevant news, and educational offerings. (Contact information, including the web site address, are noted in chapter 2.) And third, the center is a model of all-too-rare cooperation between a law school, practicing lawyers (who contributed the $1-million start-up gift to found the center), and the organized bar.

Finally, no list of accolades for the forward-thinking work of the organized bar would be complete without mention of the ABA's leadership role. Not only has the ABA sponsored publications, conferences, and studies—many of which have been cited in these pages—but its "professionalism" and lawyer assistance initiatives have been and remain on the cutting edge of what the profession needs to move successfully into the twenty-first century.

The ABA's lawyer-assistance efforts, as of this writing under the capable leadership of Dallas lawyer John W. Clark, Jr., have been particularly broad-based and effective. Contact information for those who need their services, want to inquire about or order resources, or would like to be a part of their good work:

ABA Lawyer Assistance Foundation
541 N. Fairbanks Court, 14th Floor
Chicago, IL 60611-3314
(312) 988-5359

Bravo to the good men and women in bar organizations across the country who have seen the need and generously responded with their time and resources. Together with those in law schools and firms who have risen to the challenge currently facing the profession, their efforts are a reasonable basis for encouragement. We can only hope that they are "the wave of the future," and that their ranks will be swelling by many multiples in the near term.

Notes

1. *See* HARRY T. EDWARDS, *The Growing Disjunction Between Legal Education and the Legal Profession*, 91 MICH. L. REV. 34 (1992).
2. DEREK BOK, *A Flawed System*, HARVARD MAG., May-June 1983, at 38.
3. *Id.* at 45.
4. ANTHONY T. KRONMAN, THE LOST LAWYER: FAILING IDEALS OF THE LEGAL PROFESSION (1993).
5. *Id.* at 353.
6. MARY ANN GLENDON, A NATION UNDER LAWYERS 217 (1994).
7. *Id.*
8. ROGER E. SCHECHTER, *Changing Law Schools to Make Less Nasty Lawyers,* 10 GEO. J. LEGAL ETHICS, Winter 1997, at 367, 369.
9. *Id.*
10. Professor Schiltz has since moved to the University of St. Thomas School of Law in Minneapolis, where he holds the St. Thomas More Chair and serves as Associate Dean.
11. PATRICK J. SCHILTZ, *On Being a Happy, Healthy, and Ethical Member of an Unhappy, Unhealthy, and Unethical Profession,* 52 VAND. L. REV., May 1999, at 871, 873.
12. WALTER BENNETT, THE LAWYER'S MYTH: REVIVING IDEALS IN THE LEGAL PROFESSION 187 (2001).
13. LAWRENCE S. KRIEGER, *What We're Not Telling Law Students—and Lawyers—That They Really Need to Know: Some Thoughts-in-Action Toward Revitalizing the Profession From Its Roots,* 13 J. J.L. & HEALTH 1998–99, at 1, 3.
14. *Id.* at 4.
15. *Id. at* 8–11 (capitals in headings in original; emphasis added).
16. *Id.* at 3, 12–14.
17. DEBORAH L. RHODE, IN THE INTERESTS OF JUSTICE: REFORMING THE LEGAL PROFESSION 197 (2000), citing ANN L. IIJIMA, *Lessons Learned: Legal Education and Law Student Dysfunction,* J. LEGAL EDUC., 1998, at 48.
18. For a full report of the findings, *see* G. ANDREW H. BENJAMIN, *et al.*, *The Role of Legal Education in Producing Psychological Distress Among Law Students and Lawyers,* 1986 AM. B. FOUND. RES. J. 225.
19. *Id.*
20. *Id.* at 236. *See also* G. ANDREW H. BENJAMIN, *et al., The Prevalence of Depression, Alcohol Abuse, and Cocaine Abuse Among United States Lawyers,* 13 J.L. & PSYCHIATRY 233 (1990).
21. *See* text in chapter 4 at notes 23–28.

22. BENNETT, *supra* note 12, at 18.
23. *Id.*
24. *Id.* at 26–27.
25. *Id.* at 172.
26. RHODE, *supra* note 17, at 185–86.
27. *Id.* at 198.
28. AMERICAN BAR ASS'N, THE PULSE OF THE PROFESSION 37 (Nov. 22, 2000).
29. *Id.*
30. *Id.*
31. *Id.* at 43.
32. SCHILTZ, *supra* note 11, at 936, citing CYNTHIA COTTS, *Largest Provider of Loans to Law Students Pushes New Frugality,* NAT'L L.J., Jan. 12, 1998, at A14.
33. BENNETT, *supra* note 12, at 4.
34. GLENDON, *supra* note 6, at 90.
35. RHODE, *supra* note 17, at 27 (internal quotation and footnote omitted).
36. AMERICAN BAR ASS'N, *supra* note 28, at 23.
37. *Id.*, p. 43.
38. *See* SCHECHTER, *supra* note 8, at 386–87, extolling the wisdom of Harvard's loan-forgiveness program for graduates who choose to pursue lower-paying public service jobs.
39. *Id.* at 370–93.
40. *Id.* at 376.
41. *Id.*
42. *Id.* at 379.
43. *Id.* at 382.
44. *Id.* at 383.
45. *Id.* at 387.
46. *Id.* at 387–88.
47. *Id.*
48. *Id.* at 393 (footnotes omitted).
49. *Quoted in* RHODES, *supra* note 17, at 185.
50. *Quoted in* LAWRENCE M. FRIEDMAN, HISTORY OF AMERICAN LAW 606 (2d ed. 1985).
51. *Id.*
52. *Id.* at 612–17.
53. *Id.* at 618–19.
54. *Id.* at 619.
55. For a description of efforts and programs at Northeastern and Suffolk law schools, *see* STEVEN KEEVA, TRANSFORMING PRACTICES: FINDING JOY AND SATISFACTION IN THE LEGAL LIFE 178–79 (1999).
56. BENJAMIN SELLS, THE SOUL OF THE LAW: UNDERSTANDING LAWYERS AND THE LAW 105 (1994).

57. *See* the text in chapter 3 at notes 72–78.
58. Ms. Greenberg's work is discussed, and the address and phone number of Lawyers in Transition are noted, in chapter 2 at note 115.
59. *Id.*
60. BREAKING TRADITIONS: WORK ALTERNATIVES FOR LAWYERS (Donna M. Killoughey ed. 1993), at 294.
61. *Id.* at 26–27.
62. *Id.* (emphasis added).
63. AMERICAN BAR ASS'N, *supra* note 28, at 31.
64. *Id.* at 8.
65. BENNETT, *supra* note 12, at 180.
66. *Id.* at 181.
67. PRESTON K. MUNTER, M.D., *Law Firm Policies and Procedures to Reduce Stress, in* LIVING WITH THE LAW: STRATEGIES TO AVOID BURNOUT AND CREATE BALANCE 69–79. (Julie M. Tamminen ed., Amer. Bar Ass'n 1997).
68. *Id.*; *see also* MARTHA M. PETERS's chapter, *Teaching Stress Management in the Law Office,* at 61–67; Peter Kutulakis, *Stress Management Checklists,* at 81–83, in the same publication.
69. HEMAN A. MARSHALL III, *An Introduction to the VBA Law Practice Management Division,* VA. B. ASS'N NEWS J., Apr. 2002, at 6.
70. *Id.*
71. *See* text in chapter 2 between notes 79 and 80.
72. For a summary of the work of these two South Carolina organizations, *see* J. ROBERT TURNBULL JR., *Lawyers Helping Lawyers: Help When You Need It,* S. C. LAW., Sept./Oct. 2002, at 15; ROY T. STUCKEY, *Law School Center Tackles Professionalism Issues,* S. C. LAW., July/Aug. 2002 at 21.
73. TURNBULL, *supra* note 72, at 16.
74. *Id.*

CHAPTER 6

Parting Thoughts: Practicing Law in the New Millennium

My father's obituary was full of impressive achievements and accolades: A successful trial lawyer who entered the corporate world and retired as Chairman and Chief Executive Officer of Duke Power Company, then the area's largest employer. Named by *Financial World* magazine "Chief Executive of the Year" for the utility industry in 1977, and one of the ten outstanding CEOs of all major U.S. corporations in 1980. Chosen in 1982, the year he retired, by the *Wall Street Transcript* as the top CEO in the electric utility industry. Former president of the statewide chamber of commerce group, the North Carolina Citizens Association, which honored him as the state's "Man of the Year" after he retired. And a member of too many corporate and nonprofit boards and recipient of too many lesser awards to mention here.

I loved and admired my father, but I remember another side to all this "success," as most of us are tempted to define and desire it. I remember, for example, a cold February afternoon when I was fourteen, in 1966, when I arrived home from school to learn my mother had put a bullet through her heart. I remember football games and wrestling matches my father was too busy to make. I remember the struggles with alcohol, the tension in our family even on vacation, and the lack of real warmth in our relationship as we tried to build as adults what he had been too busy or preoccupied to build while I was growing up.

I do not mean to overstate the case. Carl Horn, Jr., after whom I was named, took good care of his family. All four of his children were challenged to pursue excellence, to be "well-rounded," to be scrupulously honest, and to give back to their world more than they took from it.

Like many southern fathers, he taught his boys to hunt and fish. We had a place at the lake, where we learned to water ski (one of us barefoot) and spent many mostly pleasant weekends. All four children received excellent educations and have done well as adults. Two years after my mother tragically took her life, he married a wonderful woman who remains a central figure in our lives.

Yet that really is not the whole story of our family, or of many other families that look successful from the outside, either. And it is what was missing—deep heart connections that take time and priority attention to develop—that has most motivated me as an adult. It began to motivate me, I think, that cold February afternoon in 1966. It motivated me to marry my life partner in 1972, and to make it a priority to keep working on our relationship for all these years. It motivated my career decisions, leaving at one point a successful, growing law firm to work for several years in a college development office and later in government. It continues to motivate me as a father, husband, boss, and friend. And it motivated me to write this book.

I hope it comes through in these pages how much I love the law and the legal profession. In addition to my father, both my uncles were lawyers for whom I had great admiration and respect. My early impression of what it means to be a lawyer came more from them than from my father, who left practice for the corporate world when I was still young. One of my uncles, who had no children of his own, put more than a dozen kids through college while he was alive and endowed the largest scholarship at a major university when he died. Back in the days when most lawyers handled both civil and criminal matters, I recall as a boy going with him to the jail on Sunday nights to visit clients who had landed there over the weekend. Although he was a self-made man worth millions when he died, there were lots of clients he represented throughout his career for very little or nothing. When I read about Atticus Finch, I still think of him, my Uncle Guy Carswell.

My other uncle was a southern judge with a passion for civil rights and justice before it was politically correct or even much on people's minds—at least in Montgomery, Alabama, where he lived and held court. I recall sitting in his courtroom during our long summer visits to my mother's hometown, awed by his wisdom and balance. For the violent, career criminal, the worst news of all was that their case had been assigned to Judge Richard Emmet, but I also remember his gentleness and genuine concern for those who needed more compassion and guidance than harsh punishment. During my years in practice, I thought of my Uncle Guy Carswell as a role model—a great example of one who understood law as a "high calling"—and I frequently think of my Uncle Dick's balance and human touch as I seek to dispense justice as a judge. Their understanding of law, like most of their contemporaries, is in stark contrast to many practitioners today, who regard and treat the law as little more than a profit-driven business.

Let's get back to our roots. Let's recognize what Dean Kronman calls our "spiritual crisis" and reclaim the "soul" he describes the profession as in "danger of losing."[1] Let's rekindle the ideals and rediscover the high calling that are our prouder heritage. And let's do it in way that is sufficiently visible and public that the average man or woman on the street will once again view law and lawyers not as greedy, unprincipled shysters, but as honorable professionals worthy of admiration and respect.

This book has attempted to bring together, as cohesively as possible, a large body of information on trends and developments spanning hundreds of years. However, unless the message is boiled down to relatively simple contemporary applications, the project will ultimately fail. Perhaps we will increase our chances for success if the intended applications are restated here.

First, that law can and should be understood and practiced as something higher and nobler than just a way to make a good living—although it is certainly that, too, and there is undeniably (and properly) a business side to the practice of law. Second, that we should reconnect with the tradition Elihu Root and others represented: the *counselor* at law. "About half the practice of a decent lawyer," Root once observed, "consists in telling would be clients they are damned fools and should stop."[2] True then, true now. Third, that as "officers of the court" lawyers should embrace ethics, principles, and values far exceeding the *de minimus* requirements of the various Codes of Professional Responsibility. Fourth, that lawyers should look for creative ways to make peace between potential disputants and provide more proactive counsel, regarding litigation as a last resort. And fifth, that the legal profession, from law school through retirement, should embrace balance and wholeness for the professional and personal life of every lawyer.

Of course this is easier said than done. Through objective review of available data we have seen that a certain percentage of our brothers and sisters at the bar are miserable. Many others are functioning in the "state of mild torpor" identified by Dr. Benjamin Sells, able to continue practicing but certainly not passionate or even enthusiastic about it.[3] Some polls and surveys indicate that a majority of lawyers would not recommend that their own children follow in their professional footsteps.[4]

I *would*—but only if my children approached and embraced LawyerLife with knowledge of its contemporary pitfalls, and with clear priorities and a commitment to good time management (Steps 1 through 3). And if they recognized the importance of maintaining healthy lifestyle practices, living beneath their means so as to never become "wage slaves,"[5] and of not letting technology control their lives (Steps 4 through 6). Assuming they were still heeding Dear Old Dad's advice, I would remind them that their character was of central importance and should never be compromised, to "just say no" to some clients, and to protect their emotional health (Steps 7 through 9). And finally, I would encourage my lawyer children to embrace their profession as a "high calling," to be generous with their time and money, and to pace themselves for a "marathon" (Steps 10 through 12).

Assuming I was successful in persuading one of my children to pursue a legal career, it certainly would be nice to entrust their legal education and training to a law school where these points and principles were affirmed. A law school where the faculty and administration worked together to produce healthy, ethical, well-balanced lawyers—where not just an occasional voice, but the average professor really cared about the life and professional world into which the students were graduating. And we would expect the curriculum, programs, and opportunities of the law school to clearly reflect it.

And once these proverbial children of ours graduated from law school, wouldn't it be great if there were enough law firms that shared this high and balanced view of the law to employ them? Law firms where high-quality legal services were a given, but balanced priorities remained intact from top to bottom. Law firms where experienced lawyers "took under their wing" the inexperienced ones, where billable hours requirements (if any) were counterbalanced with genuine concern for the holistic development of the professional person, and where workaholism is seen as much of a threat to success—properly defined—as any other harmful addiction. And, of course, law firms where steps are taken to reduce the stress inherent in a rigorous professional life to reasonable and manageable levels.

Someone pinch me. I think I have been dreaming.

A Word About Women

As noted in chapter 1, the practicing bar remained remarkably undiversified into the mid-twentieth century. From the most prestigious firms in major metropolitan areas to solo practices in small-town America, the legal profession was a largely white male fraternity. Recall Mary Ann Glendon's interview in the early 1960s at Cravath, Swaine & Moore, and you will get the flavor. Then a top graduate of an elite law school (and now a distinguished Harvard law professor), Glendon's gender was an insurmountable hurdle. "I couldn't bring a girl in to meet Tom Watson [of IBM] any more than I could bring a Jew," the partner had crudely explained.[6]

But, as it turned out, a new day was dawning. Beginning in the 1960s, the percentage of women in entering law school classes increased, gradually at first and then more dramatically. By the late-1970s, the percentage of women entering law school was roughly a third of each class; early in the new millennium it is approximately half. As increasingly diverse law school classes have graduated, the percentage of women in practice has risen accordingly.

But while the numbers have dramatically grown, the experience of women in the profession remains a work in progress. Although the situation has improved somewhat, women entering this formerly male-dominated world have not uniformly found fulfillment there. Two surveys of women lawyers, as reported by *Working Women* magazine in April 1993, are instructive in this regard. In response to a question about whether respondents would choose law as a career again, the percentage answering "yes" dropped from 92 percent in 1967 to 54 percent in 1993. According to *The Wall Street Journal* article on the 1993 survey, the number-one reason given by the women answering "no" was "the competitive and acrimonious atmosphere in many law firms."[7] In other words, many women were understandably uncomfortable in an atmosphere dominated by traditional male qualities and characteristics.

As Stanford Law Professor Deborah Rhode notes, another reason female lawyers are more stressed and unhappy than their male counterparts is the tension between professional advancement and the practical reality that "employed women . . . still spend about twice as much time on domestic responsibilities as employed men."[8] In spite of the enlightened ideal of equally shared home and family responsibilities, this means for many women a choice between "sweatshop schedules [as a] full-time attorney" and "glass ceilings for part-time practitioners." Those with the greatest family commitments often drift off the partnership track, leaving behind a decision-making structure insulated from their concerns. Such patterns help account for the underrepresentation of women in positions of greatest professional status and reward."[9]

Deborah K. Holmes explores "Work-Family Stress" in her contribution to *Living with the Law: Strategies to Avoid Burnout and Create Balance.*[10] A graduate of Harvard College and Law School, Ms. Holmes's observations and suggestions are grounded in more than a decade of consulting with businesses "wishing to capitalize on the talents of all their employees, including women and others who need to balance professional and personal lives."[11]

Noting that "plans to change jobs are more than twice as common among women lawyers (51 percent) as among men lawyers (22 percent)" and that "[w]omen lawyers experience work-family stress to a greater extent than men lawyers do,"[12] Holmes makes a number of insightful suggestions for the sensitized employer. More law firms should make an effort to implement these suggestions, which include "meaningful part-time work"; "job-sharing arrangements"; "telecommuting"; and entry, exit, and reentry into the full-time work force based on the increasing and then decreasing demands of "child-rearing and [corresponding] life cycles."[13]

Holmes' suggestions are consistent with the hopeful predictions made in 1989 by Steven Brill, publisher of *The American Lawyer,* about the future of women in the profession. Writing in his own publication, Brill predicted that by 2000, law firms would be embracing flexible work arrangements for women attempting to balance work and family:

> Remember, again, that the talent hunt will be the chief problem facing the law firm of the future, and you'll have no trouble agreeing that these firms will self-interestedly become leaders in accommodating women into the business world. With women now making up some 40 percent of the law school graduating classes and with technology allowing most work to be portable, flextime, part-time, and other types of arrangements

> will become routine. Moreover, as women truly gain equal status, firms will begin to accommodate the husbands in two-career families in the same way.
>
> As a paper-based professional service business, the law lends itself almost uniquely to part-time working arrangements, and the smartest firms will find that their product-supply crisis can be stemmed by being as flexible as possible. In fact, some will develop programs for seeking out women who have left practice at their firms or equivalent firms to raise families in order to encourage them to reenter the profession.[14]

Although Brill's timing was off, let us hope that his optimistic prognosis will ultimately prove prophetic.

We do not succumb to gender stereotype by recognizing practical reality: More women than men suffer discomfort over being torn between work and family.[15] Indeed, by denying these recurring tugs of the female heart—which is a wonderful and commendable thing, not something to be denied or suppressed—we only prolong the legal profession's pressing need to catch up with the business world in finding more creative ways to achieve better balance.

Professor Walter Bennett makes an important corollary point in *The Lawyer's Myth: Reviving Ideals in the Legal Profession*, namely, that the legal profession needs to embrace what have traditionally been regarded as "feminine" qualities as much as female lawyers need the profession to accommodate their legitimate concerns.[16] Drawing heavily on Jungian psychology—in which every person, irrespective of gender, is understood to have a masculine and feminine side—Bennett identifies "the [h]istorical [m]asculinity of the [p]rofession" as problematic.[17] He explains:

> "Masculine" in its pure form includes: (1) Characteristics that are associated with the rise of *logos*, the ascendance of the rational as a way—*the* way—of problem solving. Its thought is both *linear*, moving carefully step by step to an assumed (or even fore-sighted) conclusion, and *abstract*, which manifests in a tendency or even compulsion to disembody thought from context—particularly contexts which engender emotion. As we have noted, this type of thinking is essential to legal practice and to competence as a lawyer. (2) Characteristics associated with force, physical power, and linear energy—power that can smash through things, overcome them, or drive through them. Often this is the power lawyers feel they need to win. (3) Characteristics that tend to value individuality and independence over relationships, interdependence, and mutual

> obligation. And (4) characteristics that promote and respect structure—often hierarchical structure—and order.
>
> "Feminine" in its pure form includes: (1) Characteristics associated with the rise of *mythos*, which exalts narrative over abstract logic. Its thought processes and decision-making are thoroughly embedded in context. It is holistic and inclusive and resists pure abstraction and linear delineation. It accepts emotion as an important part—and sometimes the most important part—of the context in which decisions are made. (2) Characteristics associated with accommodation and acceptance rather than raw force and power, and characteristics associated with compromise and conciliation rather than winning. These are also qualities essential to law practice, although they have frequently not been recognized as such. (3) Characteristics that base their power in relationship building, empathy, and mutual understanding rather than independence and use of individual force. These characteristics are elemental in building a profession. And (4) characteristics of inclusion and acceptance and of seeing things as a sometimes amorphous, complex, and interrelated whole, rather than as ordered, logically structured, and ranked hierarchically.[18]

The reader will notice the clear connections between Professor Bennett's description of the "feminine" side of human experience and the twelve steps recommended in chapter 4. The importance of relationships, solid priorities, peacemaking, and emotional health and balance are all squarely within what Bennett identifies as the "feminine in its pure form."[19] It is precisely these characteristics and qualities that have been difficult for the legal profession, and many individual lawyers, to sustain.

"In Jungian terms," Bennett concludes, we are a profession with "a psyche out of balance. And, indeed lack of balance—or temperance and reasonable measure—is at the heart both of the public approbation of lawyers and of the moral and emotional malaise afflicting the profession. . . . It is not surprising that many lawyers are unhappy in their work or that there is an ethical crisis in the profession. The most humane part of lawyers' characters, the parts which give life meaning, connection, and moral purpose, have been systematically repressed and excluded."[20]

Viewed this way, what has been regarded as a problem—accommodating female lawyers on the so-called "Mommy Track"—presents as an opportunity for professional growth and development. Everyone wins. The legal profession regains its psychic and emotional balance, reconnecting with elements of human experience "which give life meaning, connection, and moral purpose."[21] Women lawyers who choose for a period to devote more of their time and energy to family are accommodated and certainly not penalized for following their hearts. Indeed, male lawyers with families would do well to follow their commendable example.

Work Arrangements Have Consequences

The ABA's 2000 "Pulse Study" noted what it called "a sort of renaissance movement underfoot towards reestablishing law as a more personal and professional endeavor."[22] Motivated by "lawyers who have consciously opted for a career of less pressure and greater intrinsic rewards," these lawyers are reportedly:

- Living and practicing in smaller cities;
- Joining firms with a "family-friendly" culture;
- Starting their own firms;
- Changing career to in-house counsel or public law positions, with more regular hours; [and]
- Working part-time, with the related consequence for advancement.[22]

How widespread these trends are is "unclear," but the Pulse Study described it as "critical" for those seeking to understand the contemporary legal profession "to recognize . . . that many lawyers [now] define success in terms of overall quality of life."[23] Recalling recurring comments in the focus groups on which the ABA report was based, the authors noted that "[m]ost of the [participating] lawyers . . . don't distinguish between 'personal goals' and 'career goals.' Instead, they [now] have 'life goals.'"[24]

Lawyers of all ages and stages of practice who participated in the focus groups affirmed "the importance of living a more balanced life."[25] To illustrate this point, the report quotes three lawyers, categorized as a "New Bar Admittee," a "Firm Decision-Maker" and a "Female Class V Lawyer."[26] The reported comments certainly appear to support the larger proposition. "[W]hat do I really want?" the New Bar Admittee rhetorically asked. "I want quality of life. I don't want to have to go some place and bill my life away."[27] The Firm Decision-Maker, although more philosophical in focus, appeared supportive. "You'll look back and remember what you missed," he conceded, "not the deal that made you miss it."[28] And the older female lawyer agreed: "I guess I'm willing to take a lot less money because of my personal goals. I like my sanity. I have hobbies. I'm a big runner. . . . I don't have family commitments right now, but I do have a social life. I want to have time for myself. . . . I want to have a happy medium."[29]

Sentiments like these, and the realization that work arrangements generally have clear and unavoidable quality of life consequences, are leading some lawyers to choose nontraditional alternatives. While a majority still go the traditional route—full-time positions with law firms—an increasing number of lawyers are choosing other work arrangements.

The ABA's Section of Law Practice Management has done an excellent job in cataloguing and describing the creative work arrangements that seem to be emerging. A complete list of ABA publications, including those on this rapidly evolving topic, is available from:

ABA Publishing
American Bar Association
321 N. Clark St.
Chicago, IL 60610
(312) 988-5000
web site: http://www.ababooks.org

Two publications of the Section of Law Practice Management on the subject of alternative work arrangements—liberally quoted and cited—also deserve special mention here. They are *Breaking Traditions: Work Alternatives For Lawyers*, edited by Donna M. Killoughey and published in 1993, and *Living with the Law: Strategies to Avoid Burnout and Create Balance*, edited by Julie M. Tamminen and published in 1997. Drawing on over 50 authors from a broad range of backgrounds, these compilations are a rich introduction to alternative work arrangements that may be emerging. Subjects covered include part-time work, flextime, project lawyers, contract lawyers, cost and compensation issues, job sharing, issues relating to partnership, the "Mommy-Tracking Mentality," of-counsel arrangements, telecommuting and other technology-related issues, and in-house counsel positions.

Work arrangements do indeed have quality-of-life consequences. Only individual lawyers or law firms can determine what best suits their needs at a particular time or stage of practice. However, being aware of the implications and consequences of choices is a step in the right direction no matter what those choices turn out to be.

How About a Sabbatical?

"It took my leaving a job I loved for a one-year sabbatical," writes California State Bar General Counsel Diane C. Yu, "for me to appreciate why the academic profession has supported the notion for so long."[30] Like many contributors to the ongoing LawyerLife conversation, Yu's decision to take a sabbatical certainly was not motivated by lack of career success. Educated at Oberlin College and U.C. Berkeley School of Law (Boalt Hall), Yu was named one of the Ten Outstanding Young Women of America in 1985, served as a White House Fellow in the Executive Office of the President in 1986 and 1987, and argued and won a case before the U.S. Supreme Court in 1989.

Fortunately for this talented young woman, however, she realized before it was too late that her inner resources needed the kind of renewal a sabbatical provides. Success in our careers is an important goal, but like the man "who gains the whole world but loses his soul,"[31] professional success will produce diminishing fulfillment if all we do is work, work, work. As Ms. Yu concluded following her sabbatical, "[t]here may be no better way to enhance morale, stave off job burnout, offer fresh professional stimulation, and develop new opportunities for growth."[32]

That was certainly the experience of Columbia, South Carolina lawyer Franklin J. Smith, who recently returned from a three-month sabbatical. Rather than being "forlorn, longing for more time off, and lamenting the fact that [he] was back in the fast lane," Smith likens his renewed energies and enthusiasm for the law to "the fervor of a first-year associate."[33] Indeed, he reports, "the warm afterglow of [his] sabbatical is almost as enjoyable as the event."[34]

The terms and conditions of sabbatical programs, which are still relatively rare, differ widely among law firms that have them. Some, like Franklin Smith's, are paid. Others, like Diane Yu's yearlong sabbatical, are unpaid, requiring either substantial savings or alternative employment. At a minimum, however, lawyers on sabbatical are guaranteed employment (or continued partnership) once they return.

Like the vicarious pleasures some of us enjoy when leafing through travel magazines, Franklin Smith's account of his sabbatical—published in the March 2003 issue of *South Carolina Lawyer* under the title "Life in the Slow Lane: The Joys and Benefits of a Sabbatical"—will give pleasure to many lawyers, whether or not a sabbatical is likely to be in their futures. A litigator with 18 years of practice experience, Smith describes the joy he felt in being free for a time of "controlled anxiety" punctuated by

> sudden and unexpected flashes of terror that come in the shower, in the middle of the night or at one of my children's soccer games. Is the discovery deadline tomorrow? Did that Notice of Mechanic's Lien get filed? Was the North Lake answer due yesterday?[35]

At some point, Smith decided he would take a break from this "fast lane of too many obligations, too much pressure, and too little relaxation and reflection" and, in fact, that he "needed to spend some time in the slow lane if [he] wanted to survive the fast lane."[36] As they say, the rest is history.

The first step for Smith was to do some research. How many law firms nationally have sabbatical policies? He found no reliable data to address his question, although based on anecdotal information, it is probably safe to describe the number as "small but growing." He did identify and talk it over with a friend, Allen Gibson, a partner in a Charleston, South Carolina firm that "has had a sabbatical policy for decades."[37] His conversation with his friend only confirmed his settled intentions to make it happen.

Armed with a copy of the Charleston firm's policy, which he had revised to conform with his firm's shareholder agreement, Smith's next step was to present the proposed sabbatical policy to his firm. Although his proposal received a "tepid reception" at first, after "more than a year of discussion and minor revisions," his persistence eventually paid off and the policy was adopted.[38]

Smith's article lists key provisions in his firm's sabbatical policy and notes specific steps he took to prepare for his— beginning a year in advance—which lawyers or firms considering sabbatical policies may want to review. But I suspect most lawyer readers will most enjoy subsections in the article captioned "Adjusting to the slow lane"; "Enjoying the slow lane"; and "Reveling and reflecting in the slow lane." It is here in Smith's enviable experience that the vicarious pleasure lies and the imagination becomes most engaged.

With a touch of hyperbole, Franklin Smith gives a summary description of his three months on sabbatical as "90 days of languorous living with no commutes, no suits, no clocks, and no socks."[39] Well, not exactly—unless the planes he and his family flew on to Europe, San Francisco, and Hawaii were all caught and boarded without "clocks or socks," but it makes great poetry. And after the approximately two months of travel, including an annual vacation on North Carolina's Outer Banks with college friends and their families, perhaps "languorous living" without clocks or socks does describe the 30 days spent at home. Smith enticingly describes the month at home as being "as enjoyable and important as the two months of travel." He elaborates:

> Rarely do you get the opportunity to truly relax and enjoy yourself at home. My days were spent exercising, reading, piddling around the house, and taking naps whenever the urge struck me. I recall one day when I saw with clarity how special my sabbatical had been. It was a Wednesday morning. I was riding to Chick-fil-A to get sandwiches for lunch at school with one of my children. A Caribbean melody was wafting from the speakers, the sunroof was open and I had on my usual sabbatical attire: shorts, t-shirt and flip-flops. From nowhere I was struck by a feeling that can only be described as intense satisfaction.[41]

Now back at work, Franklin Smith concludes his account not only by reporting renewed enthusiasm for law practice, but also extolling the family memories made possible by a strategically planned sabbatical. Indeed, when he weighs the approximately 15 percent reduction in his billed fees for that year against "climbing the Eiffel Tower [with his wife and children], cruising the Seine, gazing at the Mona Lisa, touring the Tower of London, experiencing Wimbledon, taking a helicopter ride over Maui, and seeing plays in London and San Francisco,"[42] the reader can almost sense a broad smile breaking out on this happy lawyer's face.

As Ms. Yu makes clear in her less personal but equally enthusiastic account, the terms and conditions of sabbaticals—and therefore the kind of planning they require—differ widely. But whatever the specifics, Yu emphasizes the benefits not only to the one on sabbatical, but to the "[c]ompanies, law offices, and government agencies" for whom they work.[43] Depending on the particular policy, these benefits to the employer (or partners) may include "better-motivated workers, an attractive drawing card from the standpoint of recruitment and hiring, salary savings while the individual is on leave, and a returning professional or executive who has acquired new skills or refined existing ones."[44]

Sabbatical policies and programs remain relatively rare among traditional law firms, although they appear to be on the increase. Those who have taken them, like Diane Yu and Franklin Smith, frequently become almost evangelistic in their support. And for law firms concerned about balance and quality of life, it is hard to imagine a more generous or practical way to show it. Let us hope that sabbaticals, employed effectively for so many years in the academic world, is an idea whose time is about to come for the nation's overworked and stressed-out lawyers.

Parting Thoughts

Now, members of the jury, the evidence is in, and it is your turn to deliberate. You have reviewed the studies and heard the opinions of many experts. You have been introduced to the experiences of your fellow lawyers, some happy and some not so happy, and have seen what many are doing to find fulfillment in the practice of law. Along the way you have been given a great deal of historical information to put our own times, and the issues the legal profession currently faces, in a broader perspective.

Members of the jury, it is solely up to you to address the issues that have been raised, which are summarized on the verdict form I am about to give you. Please retire into your own personal and professional "jury rooms" and do your best to reach a unanimous verdict.

When you complete this form, unlike real juries, you will *not* be discharged from further service. Much to the contrary, your service on this jury is for life, or at least as long as you labor in the law. May you find the wherewithal to keep any commitments you have made, and may we all be busy and happy engaging in what the law is essentially all about: doing justice.

VERDICT FORM

1. Do you understand law as a "high calling," not just a way to make money, and will you commit to practice it that way from this point forward?

   Yes_____ No_____

2. Will you do your best to prove the cynics wrong by practicing law in an ethical and highly principled manner, never knowingly doing something that would be fodder for yet another tiresome "lawyer joke"?

   Yes_____ No_____

3. Will you do your part to improve the public's poor view of lawyers through honorable professional conduct, community and charitable service, *pro bono* work, and other public-spirited activity?

   Yes_____ No_____

4. Will you always endeavor to be more than a "hired gun," preferring the role of wise counselor, which will include "just saying no" to some clients?

   Yes_____ No_____

5. Will you practice the Golden Rule of Lawyering, treating other lawyers (and judges) as you yourself would like to be treated?

   Yes_____ No_____

6. Do you commit to caring more about character than the bottom line, more about doing what is right, than what may seem more profitable at the moment?

   Yes_____ No_____

7. Will you establish clear priorities, drawing the line at how much of you is "for sale," and strive to be there for your family and friends as well as for your clients?

   Yes_____ No_____

8. Will you take the other "12 steps toward fulfillment in the practice of law"—including practicing good time management, implementing healthy lifestyle practices, living *beneath* your means, not letting technology control your life, and striving for emotional balance and health?

   Yes_____ No_____

9. If you are an experienced lawyer, will you commit to mentoring inexperienced colleagues?

   Yes_____ No_____

10. If you are a law school professor or administrator, do you affirm your sincere concern about the life and professional world into which your students are graduating, and will you show it in the future through your teaching style and curriculum, as well as in the extracurricular programs and services your school offers?

    Yes_____ No_____

11. If you are a managing [or otherwise influential] partner in a law firm, will you do everything within your power to enable your associates and partners to live a healthy, balanced life?

    Yes_____ No_____

Notes

1. *See* text in chapter 1 at note 2.
2. *See* text in chapter 1 at note 54.
3. *See* text in chapter 4 at note 116.
4. *See* text in chapter 2 at notes 9, 39, and between notes 54 and 60.
5. *See* text in chapter 3 at notes 72–89.
6. *See* text in chapter 1 at note 42.
7. WALL ST. J., Mar. 27, 1993 at B-12.
8. DEBORAH L. RHODE, IN THE INTERESTS OF JUSTICE: REFORMING THE LEGAL PROFESSION 10 (2000).
9. *Id.*
10. DEBORAH K. HOLMES, *Work-Family Stress, in* LIVING WITH THE LAW: STRATEGIES TO AVOID BURNOUT AND CREATE BALANCE 27 (Julie M. Tamminen ed., Amer. Bar Ass'n 1997).
11. *Id.* at v.
12. *Id.* at 44.
13. *Id.* at 45–47.
14. STEVEN BRILL, *The Law Business in the Year 2000,* AM. LAW., June 1989.
15. Consider, for example, the real-life experiences of two female lawyers quoted in the ABA's report, *The Pulse of The Profession* (Nov. 22, 2000):

> I got out of law school wanting to be rich and famous. I wanted to work for a big firm, do litigation, and be in-house. Then I got pregnant my last year of law school. I passed the bar while eight months' pregnant. My whole perspective was changed. Suddenly, the ability to have a more glamorous law practice went right out the window. It became much more important for me to spend time with my family. I really love the profession but I wouldn't probably do it the way I am doing it now. You can definitely work within the profession to make it work for you. There are certain compromises to make. I'm sure I make half of what Rachel does. In return, I spend time with my two-year old and go home at 4:00 twice a week.
>
> Female Young Lawyer, Chicago, Nonmember

> I was working on a case from six in the morning until ten at night, kind of on a contract basis, about a woman that was suing the insurance company. I was doing the defense side. When she got in the automobile accident, her breast implants became misshapen. Here I am spending 18 hours a day about this subject. I am thinking to myself, Is there anything that I could be working on in the world that is less important than this?
>
> Female Young Lawyer, Sacramento, ABA Member

16. WALTER BENNETT, THE LAWYER'S MYTH: REVIVING IDEALS IN THE LEGAL PROFESSION 93–109 (2001).
17. *Id.* at 93.
18. *Id.* at 94–95.
19. *Id.* at 95 (internal quotation omitted).
20. *Id.* at 101.
21. *Id.*
22. *The Pulse of the Profession, supra* note 15, at 9.
23. *Id.* at 9, 21.
24. *Id.* at 21.
25. *Id.*
26. *Id.*
27. *Id.*
28. *Id.*
29. *Id.*
30. DIANE C. YU, *Sabbaticals: Taking a Break, in* BREAKING TRADITIONS: WORK ALTERNATIVES FOR LAWYERS 78 (Donna M. Killoughey ed., 1993).
31. *See* Matthew 16:26, Mark 8:37.
32. YU, *supra* note 30, at 78.
33. FRANKLIN J. SMITH, JR., LIFE IN THE SLOW LANE: THE JOYS AND BENEFITS OF A SABBATICAL, S.C. LAW., March 2003, at 44.
34. *Id.*
35. *Id.* at 42.
36. *Id.*
37. Personal letter from FRANKLIN J. SMITH, JR. to the author, dated Mar. 12, 2003.
38. SMITH, *supra* note 33, at 42.
39. *Id.* at 43.
40. *Id.* at 44.
41. *Id.*
42. *Id.*
43. YU, *supra* note 30, at 78.
44. *Id.*

ABOUT THE AUTHOR

Carl Horn III has served as a U.S. Magistrate Judge for the Western District of North Carolina since 1993. A former Chief Assistant U.S. Attorney (1987–1993), Judge Horn spent the first eleven years after law school graduation in private practice and as counsel to two national non-profit organizations. He is the author of numerous books and articles, including the *Fourth Circuit Criminal Handbook*, now in its 10th edition, and is a frequent speaker at CLE and other bar-related functions.

Judge Horn and his wife of 31 years, Patricia Murphy Horn, live in Charlotte, North Carolina. They have six children, ages 12–26 (Patrick, Courtney, Brendan, Mary Ellen, Peter, and Kathryn). His activities include exercising, reading, and traveling. Judge Horn has coached youth wrestling and soccer, served as a mentor and speaker in the public schools, and as a judge in the state's Mock Trial Program for high school students. He is currently President of the countywide Coalition for Youth Wrestling and is on the board of directors of the Charlotte Pregnancy Care Center.

Author Contact Information:

Hon. Carl Horn III
United States Courthouse
401 West Trade St., Suite 238
Charlotte, North Carolina 28202
(704) 350-7470
e-mail: chorn@ncwd.net

INDEX

Order Additional Copies of

LawyerLife
Finding a Life and a Higher Calling in the Practice of Law

Mail orders to:
ABA Publication Orders
P.O. Box 10892
Chicago, IL 60610-0892

Phone orders to (800) 285-2221
Fax credit card orders to (312) 988-5568
E-mail orders to: abasvcctr@abanet.org

Please send me __________ copies of *LawyerLife: Finding a Life and a Higher Calling in the Practice of Law* (Product Code 1610024)

$30.00 Regular price
$25.00 ABA Member Price

For *Bulk Order Pricing,* Call (800) 285-2221; ask for Sharron Jones **(Product Code 1610024)**

$______ Subtotal

$______ Tax (D.C. Residents add 5.75%; IL Residents add 8.75%; MD Residents add 5%)

$______ Postage/Handling (orders up to $49.99 add $5.95, $50 - $99 add 7.99, $100+ add $9.95)

$______ **TOTAL**

***Billing* Address:**

Name: ____

Address: ____

City/State/Zip: ____________________________________

Phone Number: ___________________________________

Email Address: ___________________________________

***Shipping* Address (If different):**

Name: ____

Address: ____

City/State/Zip: ____________________________________

Phone Number:

____

Email Address: ___________________________________

Method of Payment:

______ Check enclosed payable to the American Bar Association

______ VISA

______ MasterCard

______ American Express

Account # ______________________________

Expiration Date __________________________